Helping Others

HELPING OTHERS:

A Guide to Selected Social Service Agencies and Occupations

COMPILED AND EDITED BY

NORMA HAIMES

THE JOHN DAY COMPANY / NEW YORK

An Intext Publisher

Library of Congress Cataloging in Publication Data

Haimes, Norma.
  Helping others.

  Bibliography: p.
  1. Social service—United States. 2. Social
service—United States—Directories. 3. Social
work as a profession. I. Title
HV91.H26   361'.973   73–7411
ISBN 0–381–98249–1
ISBN 0–381–90011–8 (pbk.)

The John Day Company, 257 Park Avenue South, New York, N.Y. 10010.

Published on the same day in Canada by Longman Canada Limited.

. Printed in the United States of America

Dedicated to my family:
Ida
Arthur
Patricia
Gregg
Norma Beth
Perry
David

Contents

Contents

PART II   Federal Agencies

PART III   State Agencies

Contents

Helping Others

Introduction

Purpose and Scope of the Guide

This *Guide* is intended as a starting point. Its basic purpose is to describe the wide variety of agencies and occupations that exist whose goals are to ameliorate or eradicate the social problems that confront us today. And "social problems" has been defined, in this *Guide,* in the broadest possible sense in order to include areas that are of concern to the many as well as to the few. For the individual who wants to turn *concern* into *action* and *commitment,* this *Guide* offers a needed first step: an opportunity to learn about the many and various ways an individual can reach out to help his or her fellow men.

To obtain this overview of social service agencies and occupations, 1,024 questionnaires, requesting data on current programs and relevant occupations, were sent out during an eight-month span of time—from September, 1971, through April, 1972. Questionnaires were sent to 513 private agencies, 125 federal agencies and 386 state agencies. To insure coverage of all areas of social concern, every effort was made, when possible, to contact three or more agencies having similar programs or social problem coverage. Fortunately, there are very few agencies that focus their efforts on a specific or limited area so that they are the sole representative in the field. It is more common to find one of the following: a national organization, concerned with a specific problem, with affiliates located in several cities; a large agency, with or without local offices scattered throughout the country, dealing with a wide range of social problems; or an unrelated but nationwide network of small agencies coping with newly recognized problems and concerns. Replies were received from 329 private agencies, 97 federal agencies, and 228 state agencies. From this large pool of informaton, and based on the

1

nature of the materials received, a representative selection of agencies, with the occupations pertinent to their goals, was made.

To reduce the inevitable outdating of information which occurs because of the lapse of time between the publication date of a directory of this kind and the start of its research, most of the agencies selected for inclusion have been functioning for many years. The few that were formed within the past three years are expressive of the new concerns facing society; their representation, therefore, was considered of major importance. In addition, since the main purpose of this *Guide* is to provide a comprehensive survey of the kinds of agencies and occupations which help others, emphasis on currency of the materials becomes secondary. More importantly, the information in the *Guide* can serve as a resource tool for the young person who wants to choose a career that will offer the rewards of helping others; it can serve as a stimulus to dedicated individuals who can develop similar and needed programs in their communities; or it can serve as a catalog of ideas for organizations that are contemplating revision or expansion of their activities. Further, the list is a representative sampling from a multitude of agencies with similar programs and occupational opportunities that can be located either through the local telephone directory or by examining, at a library, one of the many directories or periodicals described in the bibliography found in Part IV of this *Guide*.

The descriptive entries for the private, federal, and state agencies contained in this *Guide* include data that were provided in one form or another by the agencies and have been included here in good faith. Within each entry material has been presented in a standardized sequence to permit easy access to specific areas of information. Editorial changes have been made in the copy submitted only to assure this consistency in format. In a few cases, copy has been left unedited either by request or because it reflected the unique character of a particular agency.

Organization of the Guide

The *Guide* is divided into five parts: Parts I, II, and III contain the descriptive entries of the private, federal, and state agencies concerned, directly or indirectly, with present-day social problems.

PART I—Private Agencies—is an alphabetical listing of 74 secular, religious, and international agencies. The religious organizations described here sponsor projects in many fields, including: health, education, conservation, and community service.

With the exception of a few agencies, which have been included because current needs demand that the special nature of their activities be represented, no attempt has been made in this *Guide* to list agencies that offer only volunteer service opportunities. Instead, the occupations described or listed in Parts I, II, and III are salaried and these salaries range from those that are on a subsistence level to those that are highly competitive.

PART II—Federal Agencies—is an alphabetical listing of 27 federal agencies and programs. Entries are preceded by an introductory section entitled General Information on Careers in the Federal Government. Executive departments of cabinet rank are listed first after this special section; individual agencies within each department are listed in alphabetical order. Independent agencies appear second; and relevant programs within ACTION are described separately. Last, the U.S. Commission on Civil Rights appears.

PART III—State Agencies—is a listing of 44 state agencies and programs. This section is arranged alphabetically by state; and within states that have two or more agencies, described entries are alphabetical by agency name. The reader will find that the agency functions and occupations described in this section can be found in a similar agency or as part of the structure of a larger agency in all states.

PART IV—the Bibliography—is a listing of helpful publications —directories, career guides, pamphlets, and periodicals. It is intended as an extension of the main body of the *Guide* and as a source for further information.

PART V is comprised of two indexes. The first is an index of agencies classified according to function; the second is an index to the various occupations or position titles found in each entry. In the Function Index, agencies are listed under one or more appropriate headings; private agencies are listed first, federal agencies second, and state agencies appear last. These indexes are provided to direct users to those agencies and occupations that may be of special interest to them.

All entries in Parts I, II, and III include information on the nature and purpose of the agency; a general overview of the kinds of relevant occupations or position titles found within each agency, with salary, training, and place of assignment given when available; where to write for further general or employment information; and the sequence numbers for titles listed in the bibliography that contain the names and addresses of similar agencies.

Future editions of this *Guide* will update, where necessary, the data now contained in each entry, and will attempt to include a greater representation of agencies and occupations for areas that should have broader coverage.

Grateful acknowledgment is made to Dean Nasser Sharify who allowed me to begin this guide as a special research project during my last semester at the Pratt Institute Graduate School of Library and Information Science. I also wish to thank Professor Anne Kelly, my faculty adviser for this research project, for her advice and encouragement. In addition, particular gratitude is due to the many members of the agencies included in this book who prepared or compiled the materials contained herein. Without their help, this *Guide* would not have been possible.

NORMA HAIMES

PART I

Private Agencies

Agricultural Cooperative Development International (ACDI)

Nature and Purpose: Agricultural Cooperative Development International (ACDI) is a nonprofit, educational, consulting, and technical business organization created by leading cooperative organizations of the United States to respond to the needs of cooperatives and governments in the developing countries for assistance in management, operations, planning, organization, information, and member involvement. ACDI is made up of 26 regional and national cooperatives and national membership organizations. These large farmer-owned agri-businesses provide resources for specific project requirements. In addition, this broad base provides a vehicle for direct cooperative assistance to overseas counterpart organizations.

ACDI advises and consults in the organization and operation of agricultural cooperatives and credit in the less developed countries. Assists USAID missions in developing and implementing programs of technical assistance. Advises government institutions in agricultural marketing, supply, and credit through development of policies which strengthen such business operations and lead to procedures which enable farmers themselves to participate fully in management and eventual ownership. Carries out feasibility studies for specific cooperative ventures. Arranges formal and on-the-job training in cooperative theory and practices for government officials, cooperative functionaries, and rural leaders. Conducts technical assistance programs—both short and long term—tailored to the cooperative and credit needs of the developing countries. The organization has been or is actively engaged in projects, feasibility studies, training programs, and

7

consultation in the following geographic areas: Central and South America, Africa, and Asia.

Occupation Information: The ACDI staff consists of administrative and secretarial-clerical personnel in the home office and technicians overseas with in-country assistants. Requirements for technician positions vary. Cooperative experience is most important, with pertinent language and education background following in importance. Assignments are for two years, with extensions frequent. Technicians receive two to three weeks of orientation. Liberal salary as well as in-country allowances.

Further Information—Write to: Director, Personnel and Procurement
Agricultural Cooperative Development International
1430 K Street, N.W.
Washington, D.C. 20005

Relevant Bibliography Titles: 2, 3, 6, 12, 42, 61, 69, 70, 73, 83, 102, 103.

Alaska Children's Services (ACS)

Nature and Purpose: Alaska Children's Services is composed of the following units:

Anchorage Children's Christian Home—Two service programs are provided at two cottages. One unit is run as a group home providing residential treatment services to adolescent girls. The second provides shelter care for ten children in emergency. Children for whom family life has suddenly failed are referred for care and supervision until a suitable plan to restore the child's nurturing situation is developed.

The Center for Children and Parents—The Center provides group day care and family day care for preschool children, social services to children in their own homes, and family life education.

Jesse Lee Home—Residential treatment for children with moderate to severe behavior problems and foster-family care services are offered at this facility. Four cottages each provide a complete treatment program for ten children. The Jesse Lee Home is also the corporate headquarters of Alaska Children's Services and houses the management staff.

Lutheran Youth Center—This Center offers residential treatment services to emotionally disturbed boys in the 10–14 year age bracket. It is located on a 300-acre, farm-style piece of property.

Halfway House—There are many young people walking Anchorage streets, who, with no parental support, are lonely and lost. The Halfway House program is designed to provide a bridge between the street and society for motivated young people. In the home each resident works with the other residents and the staff toward the goal of returning to an active, full participation in society with a job, an education, and an independent and positive self-image.

Support Services and Management Services—These two units offer various centralized services needed for the successful functioning of the various units of the corporation.

Occupation Information: The following occupation titles are found at the various units:
Anchorage Children's Christian Home
  Unit Supervisor—provides social work services.
  Cottage Staff—organize the daily living experience and do the all-important day-to-day therapeutic work.
The Center for Children and Parents
  Teachers—provide group day care on a full-day or part-day, year-round basis.
  Social Workers—each provides services to about 35 families; they also provide consultation and social services to children enrolled in the day care program and to their families.
Jesse Lee Home
  Unit Supervisor—provides social work services to children and their families.
  Cottage Group Counselor—the person in charge of the cottage group; responsible for the bulk of the direct work with one group of eight to ten children.
  Cottage Housemother—responsible for providing good physical care of children and maintaining a warm, attractive cottage setting.
Lutheran Youth Center
  Social Workers—supervise the overall treatment program and provide social work services to children and their parents.
  Counselors
Halfway House
  Counselors

Further Information—Write to: Alaska Children's Services
4600 Abbott Road
Anchorage, Alaska 99502

Relevant Bibliography Titles: 15, 27, 30, 32, 41, 55, 58, 67, 77.

American Council for Nationalities Service (ACNS)

Nature and Purpose: The American Council for Nationalities Service (ACNS) is a national, nonprofit organization which promotes understanding and cooperation among the many nationality and racial groups in the United States and assists immigrants to adjust to American life and become fully participating citizens. Incorporated in 1958, the ACNS began operation January 1, 1959. A merger of the American Federation of International Institutes and the Common Council for American Unity, ACNS carries forward their 53-year-old work.

More than 370,000 immigrants were admitted to the United States in 1970. Many of these newcomers need counsel and assistance with such problems as finding jobs, learning English, reuniting their families, adjusting to American life, and becoming citizens. The ACNS has member agencies or affiliates in thirty cities. As centers of service and fellowship for all nationalities, they supply the newcomer with needed information and assistance; offer a wide range of classes, cultural programs, and American contacts; extend guidance and hospitality to many international visitors and foreign students; and work for better intergroup understanding.

Services are provided by experienced, multilingual caseworkers, group workers, and community organization specialists. ACNS advises and assists its member agencies on all phases of their work through field visits, personal conferences, technical information, regional meetings, and other services.

ACNS sends educational press releases about American life and institutions and the problems immigrants face to 600 foreign-language and nationality newspapers. It supplies some 850 radio stations in 48 states which broadcast foreign-language programs with similar educational material. It maintains contact with the leading nationality organizations, encouraging them to work closely with government and community agencies. It follows legislation, issues bulletins, and works to improve immigration and naturalization law and administration.

Occupation Information: The ACNS staff consists of professional, technical, and administrative positions. These include: field directors; assistant directors; division heads; office and business managers and caseworkers. Requirements for these positions vary. However, caseworkers should have a college degree and have specialized in immigration work.

Further Information—Write to: Director of Public Affairs
American Council for Nationalities Service
20 West 40th Street
New York, New York 10018

Relevant Bibliography Titles: 10, 32, 41, 55, 67, 77.

American Field Service International Scholarships (AFS)

Nature and Purpose: Friendship and increased understanding among their fellow men have been the aims of the American Field Service (AFS) since 1914. It was founded as a volunteer ambulance service with the French armies and carried thousands of wounded in World War I. After serving again in World War II with the Allied armies it revived the idea of a peacetime program to further the basic friendship which exists among all men. In 1947 it began its new work on the teen-age level, as being most likely to accomplish the objective.

The American Field Service is a private educational organization, and it has no religious or political affiliations. AFS conducts educational exchange programs for 16- to 18-year-old students. These International Scholarships open doors which lead to understanding and friendship among the peoples of the world. Through this door pass students from 61 countries to attend American secondary schools in more than 2,800 communities for a school year of study and first-hand experience, as well as American teen-agers from practically every state to study and live with families abroad—a two-way program of seeing and showing. In this way, young citizens of the world learn to appreciate and to respect the similarities and differences of people who, though they live in different countries, have dreams and efforts similarly directed toward the goal of a peaceful and useful life.

11

Occupation Information: AFS has approximately 175 employees in its international head-quarters in New York, and another 120 in 42 offices overseas. Employees tend to be university graduates who have had two or more years of experience in teaching, social work, or in the Peace Corps, though many other backgrounds are acceptable. Overseas offices are staffed by nationals of the countries in which the offices are located. There are many specialized departments in the international headquarters, such as finance, travel, or fund raising, but the great majority of the professional staff are concerned with the selection of students, families, and schools for participation, along with extensive counseling once participation is determined. Training is given on-the-job. All United States employees work in the international headquarters in New York with the exception of three or four who may be temporarily assigned in field offices established for brief time in varying parts of the country in order to develop stronger relationships with the voluntary community committees in those areas. Salaries are comparable to those of a secondary school.

Further Information—Write to: Personnel Department
AFS International Scholarships
313 East 43rd Street
New York, New York 10017

Relevant Bibliography Titles: 15, 41, 55, 67.

American Friends of the Middle East (AFME)

Nature and Purpose: American Friends of the Middle East (AFME) has since 1951 provided services in educational counseling and placement of students, from the Middle East and Africa, seeking a college or university education in the United States.

During the past four years more than 40,000 students from thirteen countries were interviewed overseas by AMFE representatives. Staffed by experienced counselors fluent in both English and the local language, AFME's overseas offices feature complete libraries of American university and college catalogs, reference works, comparative education studies, and current information on graduate fields of study, financial aid, testing, and U.S. living costs. Complementing and supervising the overseas staff is the Educational Services Department in Washington which reviews and directs the processing of all applications accepted for AFME student programs, and administers U.S. study programs for a growing list of governments, institutions, and companies.

Occupation Information: Positions for Headquarters Educational Services Specialist assignments require a college degree; some experience in student placement or counseling is useful but not required. Overseas positions are restricted to Directors of AFME offices in the Middle East; their staff is local. Requirements include graduate or work experience in Middle East-North African affairs and some language capability. Training is given on-the-job for both specialist and director positions. Assignments are for an indefinite length of time. Salaries are competitive.

Further Information—Write to: Mr. Orin D. Parker
Executive Vice President
American Friends of the Middle East
1717 Massachusetts Avenue, N.W.
Washington, D.C. 20036

Relevant Bibliography Titles: 3, 6, 12, 15, 102.

American Heart Association

Nature and Purpose: The American Heart Association was first incorporated in 1924 in New York State. It was for twenty-four years primarily a medical organization composed of mostly physician membership which exchanged scientific and patient management information relating to the cardiovascular diseases and their resultant problems. The Association was reorganized in 1948 as a national voluntary health agency. It was at this time that the medical community joined hands with the lay public in an effort to mount a concerted attack on these diseases.

The American Heart Association is the largest national voluntary health agency solely concerned with the conquest of heart and blood vessel diseases. It now has 55 incorporated Affiliates and 127 incorporated Chapters throughout the United States including Puerto Rico. The Association has nearly two million volunteers and between 900 and 1,000 professional staff positions. The National Office and eight regional offices are established to service the various associations, coordinate their activities and those of the National Organization, and maintain an effective system of communications within the Association and with the medical, scientific, and lay publics.

The program of the American Heart Association consists of medical and scientific research conducted in established institutions throughout the country; professional education and training for medical and medical ancillary personnel; public health education programs to inform the lay public regarding heart and blood vessel matters; community service programs, which are actively organized programs in communities, such as stroke rehabilitation, rheumatic fever prevention, etc.; fund raising through public appeal in its annual Heart Fund campaign, an ongoing bequest program and a year-round memorial gift program provide the Association its income; a management and administrative function plans, coordinates, organizes, and executes all of the above.

Occupation Information: Most staff positions within the Association are geared to service the volunteers in their efforts in the above activities. These range from Executive Director positions in Affiliates and Chapters, fund raising positions, public information and public relations specialist positions, program development positions, to generalist field representatives and consultant positions throughout the country. The latter positions are usually beginning points for new staff members. Requirements for positions vary throughout the Affiliates and Chapters. However, basic knowledge or the ability to learn the skills of effective community organization, the ability to work well professionally with many kinds of people in a cross section of communities, the abilities to speak and write effectively to staff volunteer committees and groups are essential. Training is provided on-the-job. However, there are a number of in-service, out-service and continuing education opportunities available to staff members from time to time. Since the Association is organized in all fifty states and Puerto Rico, assignments might be made in any part of the country. Salaries range from around $7,000 for beginning professional generalist positions to in excess of $20,000 depending on the position requirements and location.

Further Information—Write to: Personnel Services Director
American Heart Association, Inc.
44 East 23rd Street
New York, New York 10010

Relevant Bibliography Titles: 4, 31, 32, 67, 77, 79, 110.

American National Red Cross

Nature and Purpose: The American National Red Cross is a membership organization started in 1881 and chartered by Congress in 1900. It is one of 114 internationally recognized Red Cross societies, which not only carry on nationwide and community services and programs for the welfare of people in their own countries but also are banded together through the League of Red Cross Societies to ensure effective mutual aid around the world.

The American Red Cross is the instrument chosen by the Congress to help carry out the obligations assumed by the United States under certain international treaties known as the Geneva or Red Cross Conventions. Specifically, its congressional charter imposes on the American Red Cross the duties to act as the medium of voluntary relief and communication between the American people and their armed forces, and to carry on a system of national and international relief to prevent and mitigate suffering caused by disasters. In addition, the organization conducts health and educational programs.

The Red Cross operates through a national organization made up of a national headquarters, concerned largely with matters of policy, and area offices, which operate national programs and work directly with chapters. In addition to the national organization, there are about 3,300 chapters in the United States. The chapter is the local unit of the Red Cross and carries out the various programs in the communities.

Services and programs of the Red Cross include:

Services to the Armed Forces and Veterans provides assistance to members of the United States armed forces and their families worldwide for resolving serious problems affecting morale.

Disaster Services efforts are directed toward disaster readiness and the provision of immediate emergency assistance and services as well as recovery aid to individuals and families in need as a result of disaster.

The Red Cross Blood Program provides services designed to meet the entire blood needs of a community or to supplement existing blood supplies.

The mission of Nursing Programs is to extend the normal nursing resources of the nation through the provision of health instruction and nursing services for disaster relief and community health projects.

The Red Cross First Aid, Small Craft, and Water Safety Programs are designed to create in individuals an awareness of accident causes and to teach them the skills they must have if lives are to be saved when accidents occur.

In the area of international cooperation, the American Red Cross participates in worldwide relief programs for disaster victims and works with other national societies and the international Red Cross bodies for the relief of victims of war, civil strife, and other events beyond the individual's control.

Red Cross Youth Programs provide opportunities for all young people to participate in the work of the Red Cross. The Red Cross Youth Office coordinates the activities through which young people gain a better understanding of service to others.

Occupation Information: Although the Red Cross is primarily a volunteer organization, it maintains a career staff that is responsible for the coordination and continuity of the programs as well as for certain specific services to chapters. Red Cross professional staff members generally begin their employment in the social welfare or recreation field. The basic requirement is a degree from a four-year college or university, usually with a liberal arts background, including courses in social sciences. Men and women interested in the social work field may be employed as Red Cross caseworkers in military hospitals or as Red Cross assistant field directors at military installations. There are also opportunities for employment in social work programs carried on by Red Cross chapters in communities throughout the United States. Persons interested in recreation may become recreation workers in military hospitals with the American Red Cross. These positions require worldwide mobility. Salaries range from $6,000 to $12,000. Administrative and supervisory positions carry the highest salaries.

The duties of an assistant field director include consultation on personal and family problems, aiding communication between service personnel and their families, providing information on government benefits, arranging for Red Cross financial assistance, and organizing and directing Red Cross volunteer programs and services on the installation.

In military hospitals Red Cross social workers help in planning for the patient's recovery by assisting him through social work services. Responsibilities include helping servicemen work out personal and family problems, assisting with communications between patients and their families, and assisting patients in plans for convalescent leave and in applying for government benefits.

Private Agencies

Red Cross hospital recreation workers are responsible for providing medically approved recreation services for patients. Responsibilities include developing group activities, such as games, dramatics, and music, assisting individual patients with special interests, and conducting programs in wards and in recreation areas.

The job of the Red Cross field representative includes consultative field work in assisting Red Cross chapters with the interpretation of the organization's philosophy, purpose, policies, and procedures. Duties include assisting chapters in the promotion, organization, and development of programs and activities, including fund campaigns, and working cooperatively with volunteer field staff assigned to give chapters special support.

Disaster representatives give emergency assistance at the time of disaster, assist individual families in the development of re covery plans, and serve as members of the Red Cross disaster team. Between periods of major disasters they help chapters develop preparedness plans and assist in training needed personnel.

The Red Cross also offers career opportunities in the health field. Professional nurses are employed in the Blood Program and Nursing Programs. Both programs offer employment at the community level and on the national staff. A baccalaureate degree is required for nurses employed as supervisors or in administrative positions. The Blood Program and Nursing Programs are operated only in the United States.

Nursing consultants are assigned to a territory covering from one-half of a state to two states. Duties include assisting Red Cross chapter committees in planning and administering nursing programs, teaching instructor training courses, conducting disaster training courses, and serving as liaison between Red Cross Nursing Programs and professional and civic groups.

Further Information—Write to: National Director
Office of Personnel
National Headquarters
American Red Cross
Washington, D.C. 20006

Relevant Bibliography Titles: 3,15, 31, 32, 52, 55, 67, 73, 77, 110, 112.

American Speech and Hearing Association (ASHA)

Nature and Purpose: The American Speech and Hearing Association (ASHA) was founded in 1925. It is a national scientific and professional association for speech and language pathologists, audiologists, and speech and hearing scientists concerned with communication behavior and disorders. It is a nonprofit organization governed by a Legislative Council elected by members in each of the fifty states and by an Executive Board composed of elected officers of the Association.

ASHA's goals are to encourage basic research and scientific study of human communication and its disorders; to stimulate exchange of information about human communication through conventions, publications, and other continuing professional education activities; to promote investigation of clinical procedures used in treating disorders of communication; to maintain high standards of clinical competence for professionals providing services to the public; and to encourage the development of comprehensive clinical service programs.

Occupation Information: Speech pathology and audiology is the profession devoted to helping people overcome disabilities in speech, language, or hearing, and to contribute to our knowledge of human communication processes. Speech pathologists and audiologists provide clinical services for children and adults with problems in speech, hearing, and language; conduct research to increase understanding of the processes of speech, language, and hearing; teach college or university courses in speech and hearing sciences and in the various areas related to understanding speech, hearing, and language disorders; and administer public and private programs and agencies providing clinical services, research, and professional education.

ASHA conducts a national recruitment program for the profession, which coordinates recruitment activities in state associations and provides career information services.

Further Information—Write to: American Speech and Hearing Association
9030 Old Georgetown Road
Washington, D.C. 20014

Relevant Bibliography Titles: 30, 32, 34, 41, 67, 79, 110.

Americans for Indian Opportunity (AIO)

Nature and Purpose: Americans for Indian Opportunity (AIO) is a national, nonprofit, Indian organization, with headquarters in Washington, D.C. It is governed by a 31-member Board of Directors, made up of Indians and interested non-Indians.

AIO has been established to help American Indians, Eskimos, and Aleuts establish self-help programs at the local level, to improve communications among Native Americans and with non-Indians, and to educate the general public to the achievements and the needs of Native Americans today.

Drawing upon a large bank of Indian expertise, AIO supports Indian action projects in the fields of education, health, housing, job development and training, and opportunities for Indian young people.

AIO stands for self-determination. It believes that Native Americans are entitled to equality of opportunity while still retaining the right to be different—a fundamental American ideal. AIO believes that the real meaning of self-determination is Indians operating their own programs and deciding their own options.

AIO seeks to serve as a national advocate in Washington for all Native Americans. It monitors federal agencies to assure that Indian programs are fairly and properly administered, and seeks to take advantage of federal government programs and grants which can be of benefit to Indians on a local or national scale.

Occupation Information: AIO has no specific occupation titles. Requirements for professional positions include experience on the local level working in Indian programs; a basic understanding of the objectives and goals of AIO and a sincere desire to implement these goals. Educational qualifications are flexible since AIO considers an individual's abilities and capabilities as well as his or her educational background. Locations of assignments vary according to specific projects. Salaries vary according to positions.

Further Information—Write to: Americans for Indian Opportunity
1820 Jefferson Place, N.W.
Washington, D.C. 20036

Relevant Bibliography Titles: 1, 31, 62, 81, 94, 95, 104, 105, 111.

The Arthritis Foundation

Nature and Purpose:

The Arthritis Foundation, established in 1948, is the voluntary health agency seeking the total answer—cause, prevention, cure —to the nation's number one crippling disease. It exists to help the millions of arthritis sufferers, and to help their doctors, through programs of research, patient services, public health information and education, professional education and training.

With its 79 local chapters throughout the country, the Foundation: supports research; supports training for young medical scientists and physicians; expands community services to patients and their families; and informs doctors and patients of the latest developments in arthritis.

Occupation Information:

The national headquarters office maintains a staff of specialists, divided into the following departments: Chapter Operations; Medical and Scientific Affairs; Public Relations; Development; and Finance. In addition, the Foundation employs Regional Directors and Executive Directors to head operations of its 79 chapters. Larger chapters offer career opportunities for public relations and fund raising specialists, and members of the allied health professions. Requirements and salary levels vary depending on the individual positions. Job training also varies. In most professional positions, some travel within the United States is required.

Further Information—Write to:

Administrative Assistant for Personnel
The Arthritis Foundation
1212 Avenue of the Americas
New York, New York 10036

Relevant Bibliography Titles:

4, 31, 32, 34, 67, 77, 79, 110.

Big Brothers of America

Nature and Purpose:

The Big Brother Movement came into existence on December 3, 1904. In the early years, Big Brother work was carried on entirely by laymen. Experience proved, however, that Big Brother programs were more effective if there was a working partnership between the Big Brother volunteer and a professionally trained staff.

In 1946, thirteen Big Brother associations in the United States and Canada joined forces to form Big Brothers of America, the international body which enables local units to cooperate more effectively for the general growth and advancement of Big Brother work.

The purpose of Big Brother service is to offer an individual boy the opportunity to further his growth and development through a relationship with an adult male figure, a relationship which he would otherwise not have because of the absence, either physically or psychologically, of a father in his life. A "little brother" is a boy between the ages of eight and seventeen who needs friendship, affection, advice, and someone to emulate. He may be in difficulty with the law, emotionally deprived, fatherless, isolated in an institution, or just an unhappy boy in need of a meaningful male relationship. The Big Brother is a volunteer who attempts to give of himself in a way that contributes to the boy's growth and development.

Occupation Information:

The Big Brother service is offered under the supervision of a social worker. The social worker is involved in the processes of intake, recruitment, screening, matching, and supervision. During the intake process a total family diagnosis is made and the social worker helps the parents take as much responsibility as possible. Intake is also a meaningful experience to the boy who is helped to understand, on his own level, what he is involving himself in and why he is being given the opportunity to have a Big Brother. Through the recruitment and screening processes a prospective volunteer's suitability is determined. The matching process relates to the pairing of the Big Brother and the boy, and is a major step in implementing the treatment plan which was formulated during the intake study of the boy. Supervision is directed toward helping the volunteer initiate, sustain, and strengthen a relationship with the boy. Periodically the social worker evaluates case movement to determine whether the purposes of the assignment are being realized.

Further Information—Write to:

Big Brothers of America
341 Suburban Station Building
Philadelphia, Pennsylvania 19103

Relevant Bibliography Titles:

15, 30, 31, 32, 34, 55, 58, 67, 77, 112.

Board of Missions of the United Methodist Church

Nature and Purpose:

The Board of Missions of the United Methodist Church supports several programs which are considered to be "mission" programs. The focus is to minister to the needs of people wherever they are. There are programs both in the United States and in various countries overseas. The Overseas-3 program has a three-year overseas involvement. The US-2 program is a two-year special-term mission program located in the United States and Puerto Rico.

The Overseas-3 program was started in 1948, as requests came to the Board of Missions from the church in Japan for young people to work in rehabilitation of the country. Some seventy young people were sent that year, and from then on the United Methodist Board of Missions has been sending special-term young people overseas. For the past fifteen to twenty years the Board has sent young volunteers to many countries in Asia, Africa, and Latin America.

Occupation Information:

The Overseas-3 special-termers work mainly in the professional fields: teaching, medicine, agriculture, youth ministries, and communications. The US-2 program has similar qualifications and the nature of the work is similar. Most US-2s work in community centers, schools for minority children, schools for handicapped and/or emotionally disturbed children, town and country and inner-city urban ministries. Requirements for both programs are that the participants have a minimum of a bachelor's degree. They are to be from twenty-one to twenty-eight years of age. They may be either married or single, but the Board of Missions cannot accept married couples with children. There are special training programs for both US-2s and Overseas-3s. Salaries vary. The US-2 is provided a salary of $150 a month plus housing and laundry. Overseas-3s are provided a base salary (determined by the cost of living of the country to which one is assigned—from $150 to $200, usually). He is also provided with housing, transportation, language study, and other benefits. The application process is extensive and probing since it is geared in a step-by-step manner to explore motivations, perspectives, goals, and theological grounding.

Further Information—Write to:

Board of Missions of The United Methodist Church
475 Riverside Drive, Room 1373
New York, New York 10027

Relevant Bibliography Titles:

31, 41, 59, 62, 63, 72, 73, 87, 88, 93, 102.

Boys' Clubs of America

Nature and Purpose:

Since its founding in 1860, the Boys' Club Movement has won ever growing support as a major force for good within hundreds of cities and towns. In 1956, Boys' Clubs of America was granted a U.S. congressional charter, the only boy-guidance organization so recognized in more than forty years.

Boys' Clubs of America is a national youth serving organization representing hundreds of member Boys' Clubs throughout the United States. It is governed by a Board of Directors composed of over 150 prominent and influential Americans. Through the Boys' Club Movement, needed guidance and activities are provided daily for thousands of boys, with special attention to serving the disadvantaged.

The general purpose of the Boys' Club is to promote the health, social, educational, vocational and character development of boys. Although individual Boys' Clubs vary in program, quality, and services, depending upon their resources, the following characteristics are common to all of them: It is generally located in low income areas; it has an all-boy membership; it has full-time professional leadership; no proof of good character or pledge is required from members; any boy can afford to belong since membership dues are kept low; boys of all races, religions, and color are eligible for membership; buildings are especially designed for the conduct of Boys' Club programs; it is nonsectarian; the Boys' Club is open to all of its members at any time during its hours of operation; it has a varied and diversified program; and it is guidance oriented.

Occupation Information:

There are nearly 1,000 Boys' Clubs in the United States, serving close to a million boys on a daily basis. A new club is being established on the average of one every week. These clubs employ more than 2,500 full-time professional workers who are assisted by part-time activity specialists and volunteers. Although there are variations in titles and responsibilites in individual clubs, generally the positions are classified as follows:

The Executive Director is the administrative head of the organization. He works with the Board of Directors in the formulation of policies, procedures, budgets, and programs and coordinates and supervises the Clubs' operation.

The Director has charge of a unit in a multiple-unit organization. He may work with a unit advisory board but he is directly responsible to the Executive Director.

23

The Program Director works under the Executive Director or Director and is primarily concerned with the program activities in the Club.

The Physical Director is responsible for the planning and conducting of the physical and health education, and the recreation and sports program.

The Swimming Director is responsible for the aquatic program in Clubs with swimming pools.

The Group Club Supervisor is responsible for recruiting, selecting, and training group advisers, promoting and organizing group clubs, and integrating the group club program with the total Club program.

The Educational Director is responsible for planning and organizing shops, classes, and special interest groups and stimulating interest of members in educational and cultural activities. He directs the Educational and Vocational Guidance Program.

The Social Director is responsible for the game room, special events, co-recreational and other social activities.

In addition to leadership qualities, there are two major qualifications for professional Boys' Club work—a degree from an accredited college and skills commensurate with the specific position. It is desirable that the degree be in an area related to youth work, such as education, recreation, or the social sciences, but other areas of study are also acceptable. Salaries in the field vary in accordance with budgets, size of Clubs, living costs, and community standards. Generally, starting and average salaries are commensurate with those in other youth-serving organizations.

Further Information—Write to: Director of Recruitment and Placement
Boys' Clubs of America
771 First Avenue
New York, New York 10017

Relevant Bibiliography Titles: 15, 34, 55, 58, 67, 77.

Business and Job Development Corporation (BJD)

Nature and Purpose: Business and Job Development Corporation (BJD) was organized in 1962 by a group of volunteer Negro businessmen. In recognition of BJD's history of economic and business development for minorities at the grass-roots level, the Office of Minority Business

Enterprise, in December of 1970, appointed BJD as its affiliate to serve the Pittsburgh area.

Pittsburgh's Business and Job Development Corporation exists to promote the economic, industrial, and general welfare of the Greater Pittsburgh area with emphasis on the welfare of minority groups. To achieve this end, BJD itself seeks to sponsor, develop, and expand industrial enterprises in the area and, where necessary, assists in financing proposed industrial and commercial projects. BJD assists minority individuals and organizations in acquiring, building, and owning industrial and commercial establishments.

In light of the stated present needs and projected future needs of the area, BJD sponsors and encourages educational opportunities as a means of promoting the overall economic development of Pittsburgh with particular emphasis on minority groups and the black community.

Occupation Information: Positions in the economic development aspect of BJD include front-line implementors and development specialists who promote and develop community-based projects, both commercial and industrial, to service and employ local residents. OMBE Affiliateship positions cover the areas of business counseling, financial specialties, information coordination, and management assistance coordination. These specialists provide a comprehensive range of business development services and outreach dissemination of information, business counseling in management and other areas of business operation. There are no specific age, educational or language requirements for any of these positions, but training and/or experience in business and financial matters is required. On-the-job orientation and guidance is given. Salary range is dependent on skills and experience.

Further Information—Write to: Business and Job Development Corporation
Suite 1000, 7800 Susquehanna Street
Pittsburgh, Pennsylvania 15208

Relevant Bibliography Titles: 8, 13, 81, 94, 95.

California Rural Legal Assistance (CRLA)

Nature and Purpose:

California Rural Legal Assistance (CRLA) is a statewide law firm, funded by the Office of Economic Opportunity to provide free legal services to many of California's rural poor. It was the first OEO program designed to assist farm workers, and its initial funding in May of 1966 was the largest legal services grant ever made by the OEO office. Despite strong political pressures, the program has been refunded each year since.

CRLA is a nonprofit corporation. Since its inception, the philosophy of CRLA has been to provide to the poor the same high quality of service that the wealthy client would expect from the law firm representing his interests. The poor, like the rich, are entitled to good lawyers who take the time to serve their needs. CRLA represents groups of poor people, as well as individual indigents, recognizing that poverty is a social as well as an individual problem. Those clients which CRLA has been able to serve, for it is only able to serve a fraction of those who need its services, have come to see the law as a vehicle for their betterment. The philosophy of CRLA has been and is that the poor, when served by vigorous, competent and high-minded lawyers, can have hope amidst poverty.

Occupation Information:

The CRLA staff, statewide, consists of approximately 120 persons. Relevant positions include the attorneys who handle over 10,000 civil cases a year; and investigators and community workers who act as liaisons with the various communities. The central office, in San Francisco, coordinates legal and agency matters throughout the state and houses the administrative staff for the entire organization. Requirements for positions vary.

Further Information—Write to:

California Rural Legal Assistance
1212 Market Street
San Francisco, California 94102

Relevant Bibliography Titles:

1, 14, 94, 98.

Catholic Medical Mission Board (CMMB)

Nature and Purpose:

The Catholic Medical Mission Board is a charitable nonprofit, medical relief corporation. CMMB has operated a Medical Supply Program since 1928. Through this program, medicines, instruments, and equipment are shipped to over 5,000 Catholic hospitals and clinics in Africa, Asia, and Latin America. Each year, more than 2,000,000 pounds of supplies are moved overseas. Most of the medicines are donated by the pharmaceutical industry. Instruments and equipment are contributed by physicians, dentists, and hospitals in this country. With its limited funds, CMMB purchases special medicines for overseas use. CMMB has no missions of its own but they assist any Catholic medical mission asking their help.

In addition, physicians, dentists, nurses, technicians, and paramedical personnel who volunteer their talents to help in the treatment of the sick poor are placed overseas in Mission Institutions where an urgent need exists for their talents. CMMB makes known the availability and qualifications of short- and long-term volunteers to these medical facilities. Every year some one hundred volunteers help overseas.

Occupation Information:

CMMB's Placement Program functions as a referral source for medical, paramedical, and technical personnel who offer their professional skills to aid the countless destitute sick in foreign lands. They recruit long and short term volunteers, not necessarily Catholic, for Catholic Mission hospitals and clinics in Africa, Asia, and Latin America. These men and women serve the sick poor through their medical skills. The only "ministry" required is that of their professions. After a volunteer's references are authenticated and the individual is approved for referral by CMMB's Medical Advisory Council, the qualifications and preferences of the person are matched to the needs of the Mission. Before a volunteer is formally introduced, the requirements of the hospital or clinic are thoroughly analyzed. Special attention is given to institutions where the volunteer can participate in the training of native personnel in medical skills.

Requirements include a degree in medicine, dentistry, nursing, or technology; high personal and professional standards; a congenial, well-integrated personality; endless patience and compassion; the same qualities that make a physician, dentist, nurse, or technician successful in his or her profession here at home; and the ability to improvise while maintaining acceptable medical standards.

27

Transportation costs, monthly stipend, living expenses, residence, board, and insurance are contractual matters which are usually negotiated by the volunteer and the institution. When neither can defray these expenses, attempts are made to find a sponsor here in the United States.

Further Information—Write to:
Placement Director
Catholic Medical Mission Board, Inc.
10 West 17th Street
New York, New York 10011

Relevant Bibliography Titles: 11, 12, 31, 59, 63, 72, 73, 102, 103.

Catholic Relief Services—United States Catholic Conference (CRS)

Nature and Purpose:
Catholic Relief Services, the overseas aid agency of American Catholics, is a separately incorporated organization of the United States Catholic Conference, Inc. The officers and members of the United States Catholic Conference also serve as the Board of Trustees of Catholic Relief Services. The full, official, and legal title is: Catholic Relief Services—United States Catholic Conference, Inc. For simplicity, the organization is usually referred to as Catholic Relief Services—U.S.C.C., or CRS.

Catholic Relief Services conducts programs in seventy countries of Africa, Asia, and Latin America. CRS's two major objectives are: the provision of assistance to needy persons; and assistance with the formation and development of indigenous agencies dedicated to the welfare and development of people in the developing countries. CRS carries out its activities in four principal fields: (1) the distribution of relief supplies; (2) socio-economic development and self-help programs; (3) service to refugees; and (4) disaster aid.

CRS distributes food, clothing, and medicines to people in need without regard to race or creed, through indigenous private agencies or local governmental agencies, depending upon the situation in the country concerned. Under Public Law 480, the United States Government donates foods, which are distributed in the name of the people of the United States. These foods are used for the feeding of children in schools and institutions, nutrition education programs for mothers and children, and the pay-

28

ment of partial wages for self-help work programs dedicated to community development.

Through its activities in the socio-economic field, all types of development and self-help programs are encouraged and supported. These include community development, credit unions, cooperatives, health and welfare programs, housing, savings and loan associations, and others. In addition to providing relief for the aged, the sick, orphans, and others in need, CRS provides assistance in times of disaster, and carries on long-term rehabilitation work in the post-disaster period.

Occupation Information:

CRS sends men and women to Asia, Africa, and Latin America to engage in programs of relief, welfare, rehabilitation, and development. Program Directors of CRS are responsible for the supervision of the following aspects of programs of the Agency: (a) The overall supervision of distribution of relief supplies; (b) Assisting in the creation and development of local counterpart agencies in the fields of welfare and socio-economic development; (c) The administration of relief, socio-economic development, and disaster aid programs; (d) The establishment and maintenance of relations with officials of the American embassy, local government, local agencies, and churches; (e) The periodic reporting on Catholic Relief Services' operations. Program Assistants work under and assist Program Directors in carrying out the activities described above.

Requirements include a college education or the equivalent, with at least two years of other experience, preferably with specialized training in administration, finance, or community organization. An applicant should be at least twenty-four years of age and have a speaking and reading knowledge of either French, Spanish, or Portuguese. An orientation period of two weeks is given prior to overseas assignment, and the first year overseas is considered an in-service training period. The starting base salary is usually in the area of $6,500 per annum, with added benefits.

Further Information—Write to:

Catholic Relief Services—United States Catholic Conference
350 Fifth Avenue
New York, New York 10001

Relevant Bibliography Titles:

2, 3, 6, 7, 12, 31, 59, 61, 73, 102, 103.

Center for Auto Safety

Nature and Purpose: With financial assistance provided by Consumers Union of the United States, Ralph Nader established in April of 1968 a one-room office devoted exclusively to auto safety. In January, 1970, the name Center for Auto Safety was adopted, and in June, 1970, the Center was incorporated as a nonprofit corporation in the District of Columbia. It received federal tax-exempt status in March of 1971.

The Center for Auto Safety seeks to reduce the human and economic losses wrought by the automobile and the auto industry. While other groups focus efforts on altering driver habit and highway design, the Center concentrates on vehicle design which is easier to alter than human behavior or the driving landscape. Safer vehicle design could eliminate more than three-fourths of the deaths and injuries which occur during the "second collision" when the occupant collides with a hostile vehicle interior. Thus, the Center concentrates on prevention of injuries and deaths and leaves accident prevention to the other more traditional organizations. The Center moves in several directions:

As an *auto safety advocate*, the Center monitors the activities of the governmental agency (National Highway Traffic Safety Administration) charged with regulation of the automobile industry. In issues between the government and industry, the Center participates on the public's behalf by either supporting safety standards proposed by the government or by proposing yet stricter regulations. The Center's participation takes the form of docket submissions, petitions for rule making, presentations at public meetings, and publications. Occasionally, when stronger action is required, the Center institutes legal action.

As a *consumer advocate*, the Center is working to find ways to reduce the level of unresolved consumer complaints against the auto manufacturers. The Center now stores more than 15,000 letters and is coding them according to make, model, and defect. This information has proved helpful in assisting attorneys. It also helps to shape the Center's programs.

As an *information gathering center*, the Center collects literature and statistics on automobile safety. Access to these information files, containing information on accidents, injuries, civil suits, government actions, inventions, recall campaigns, and industry activities, is open to anyone.

As a *research center*, the Center analyzes developments in the field of auto safety which in turn shape their programs. From time to time, the Center publishes articles or fact sheets on its research efforts.

Occupation Information: Relevant positions in the Center are for lawyers, engineers, researchers, and volunteers who work in all of the areas described above. The only requirements for these positions are intelligence, commitment, and the ability to be a self-starter. All training is done on-the-job, if needed. All work is done from the center. Salaries range from $45.00 per week to $80.00.

Further Information—Write to: Center for Auto Safety
P.O. Box 7250
Ben Franklin Station
Washington, D.C. 20044

Relevant Bibliography Titles: 14, 23, 71, 105, 111.

Central Committee for Conscientious Objectors (CCCO)

Nature and Purpose: The Central Committee for Conscientious Objectors (ccco) was founded in 1948 by peace, church, and civil liberties groups. It is an independent, nonsectarian, nonprofit organization. Ccco is dedicated to helping those who are confronted by the draft. They also assist men in the military who feel unable to continue in uniform, or can no longer carry arms. They believe that every man should have as much information as possible so that he can make a reasoned response to the demands made upon him. In sum, ccco provides assistance and information about a man's rights and options under the Selective Service System and the military.

Occupation Information: Relevant positions in ccco offices are: draft and military counselors; administrators; and fund raisers. There are no specific requirements for any of these positions. The counselors generally have a college education, but this is not an absolute requirement. Previous experience is not necessarily a requisite; however, it often helps. Most training is done while a person is on-the-job. Staff members are based in Philadelphia, San Francisco, Chicago, and Atlanta and do field work throughout the United States.

31

Salaries range from subsistence level up to $5,000 for most staff members. A few have higher salaries.

Further Information: Write to the nearest of the following offices:

Central Committee for Conscientious Objectors
2016 Walnut Street
Philadelphia, Pennsylvania 19103

Western Region Office CCCO
140 Leavenworth Street
San Francisco, California 94102

Midwest Region (MCDC)
711 South Dearborn Street
Chicago, Illinois 60605

Relevant Bibliography Titles: 1, 14, 105, 111.

Council of Better Business Bureaus (CBBB)

Nature and Purpose: The Council of Better Business Bureaus (CBBB) is a new national organization formed in August, 1970, by a consolidation of the former National Better Business Bureau and the Association of Better Business Bureaus International. Its dual mission is to become an effective national self-regulatory force for private enterprise and to demonstrate a sincere and visible concern for consumers.

Offices of the CBBB are maintained in New York and Washington, D.C. The Executive Office in New York maintains contact with major corporations, advertising agencies, and the media. National activities, including broad consumer education programs and voluntary self-regulation of national advertising, are administered in this office. The Operations Office in Washington coordinates the activities of the 150 Better Business Bureaus. It develops and administers programs and procedures aimed at improving and standardizing the operations of member bureaus and handles national casework, including consumer inquiries and complaints, and trade practice codes. The Washington Office also works closely with government regulatory agencies and trade associations and keeps abreast of government activities of concern to consumers and business.

The backbone of the Council is the 150-member Better Business Bureaus located throughout the country and abroad. For more than half a century, the Bureaus have been virtually the only place a consumer could find information and help. The Bureaus have more contact with consumers than any private organization addressing itself to these problems. Bureaus also develop trade practice codes with business groups and cooperate with city and state consumer protection agencies and regional offices of the Federal Trade Commission. Advertisements are checked and correction of misleading advertising is sought. Where voluntary compliance is not obtained, offenders are referred to appropriate law enforcement agencies.

Occupation Information: Cввв has developed a training cadre project in which management trainees are, in effect, an apprentice to elected Better Business Bureaus for a period of months for training as junior executives or in direct management. Requirements for this program are a degree in either liberal arts or business administration. Initial salaries are modest. Professional positions in Better Business Bureaus are in the field of department heads, often described as trade practice consultants. They are specialists in various areas of consumer business relationships such as retail, automotive, selling and finance, appliances and kindred items, investments in various items such as franchises, purchase of insurance, and credit counseling.

Further Information—Write to: Council of Better Business Bureaus, Inc.
1150 17th Street, N.W.
Washington, D.C. 20036

Relevant Bibliography Titles: 10, 14, 23, 34, 71, 77.

Florence Crittenton Home and Services (FCH)

Nature and Purpose: The Florence Crittenton Home and Services of San Francisco offers comprehensive help to single pregnant women, single mothers, their families, babies' fathers, and other related persons. Infant day care services are also available.

Services offered include: emergency housing or immediate placement in a group home for a period of assessment and planning; and residency, including a planned services program for unmarried pregnant women, who may require prenatal and/or postnatal residential care, with or without the baby; and for teenage mothers and their babies in need of a protective setting and individualized treatment for extended periods of time. The residential service program includes: individual and group counseling around personal problems, family relationships, economic need, education, vocational guidance, training, jobs, housing, and mothering; medical consultation and referral; group activities including self-government, committee work, topical discussions, education in child care and development, arts and crafts, household responsibilities and social activities; and a baby clothes and equipment exchange for single mothers and their infants. FCH also provides services for girls not in residence and living in the community.

Occupation Information:

The service staff at FCH is comprised of the following selected positions:

Intake Social Workers—handle all inquiries and represent the agency in interpretation of services to the public; interview applicants and establish eligibility; complete pre-admission collateral contracts; initiate social diagnosis and make recommendations; finalize admission arrangements; and establish fees.

Continuing Social Workers—formulate treatment plan; set goals; provide social services to girls, parents, wider family, and boyfriends; and collaborate with agencies including welfare and probation departments, and other important collaterals, such as doctors, nurses, educators, and representatives of housing authority.

All social workers at FCH have at least the academic equivalent of the M.S.W., plus experience in working with parents and children, especially adolescents; and ability to work with community agencies.

Residence Nurses—responsible for teaching health matters which affect residents; inform girls regarding prenatal and postnatal care for self and baby; instruct in child development, nursing care, and nutrition for child; and instruct in young adult and children's illnesses, prevention, and treatment.

Requirements for nurses include training in the field of nursing with special interest in pediatrics; and work experience with adolescents, young children, and their parents.

Child Care Aides—provide direct physical and emotional care of the child, including assuming responsibility for his nutrition, health, safety, learning, and over all well-being.

Requirements include experience in working with children, knowledge about infant and child care, and personality characteristics that favor work with children.

Further Information—Write to: Florence Crittenton Home and Services
850 Broderick Street
San Francisco, California 94115

Relevant Bibliography Titles: 15, 26, 27, 32, 34, 55, 58, 67, 77, 78.

Dallas Alliance for Minority Enterprise (DAME)

Nature and Purpose: The Dallas Alliance for Minority Enterprise (DAME) is a nonprofit Texas corporation, founded in March, 1970, by more than twenty public and private sector organizations, for the purpose of providing coordination and assistance to organizations and individuals involved in the creation and expansion of minority-owned and operated businesses.

DAME's programs include the following: providing management and technical assistance to minority enterprise; providing assistance to minority entrepreneurs, and potential entrepreneurs, in obtaining capital from MESBICS, banks, SBA, and other sources; serving as a clearinghouse for dissemination of information on public and private sector programs relating to minority economic development; and sponsoring and participating in workshops, seminars, and other meetings for the improvement of minority economic development in Dallas and the Southwest. In addition, DAME is affiliated with the Office of Minority Business Enterprise.

Occupation Information: The professional staff position vital to the succcess of DAME's programs is that of the Business Coordinator/Analyst who functions in all of the areas described above. Requirements for this position include an M.B.A. and fluency in Spanish. Salaries are competitive.

Further Information—Write to: Dallas Alliance for Minority Enterprise
P.O. Box 6228
Dallas, Texas 75222

Relevant Bibliography Titles: 13, 81, 95.

Direct Relief Foundation (DRF)

Nature and Purpose:

The work of the Direct Relief Foundation (DRF) began in 1945 when William Zimdin, a refugee from Estonia, started sending medicines and clothing to displaced persons in Europe. Since that time some 1,600 hospitals in Latin America, Southeast Asia, the Far East, and Africa have been helped by DRF. Annually DRF's Medical Relief International Program channels millions of dollars' worth of donated drugs and medical equipment to hospitals and clinics in remote sectors of the world. The number of patients receiving medicines or food supplied by DRF runs into the millions every year. Not all of them are in hospitals; medical care is also administered under emergency field conditions. DRF each year meets requests for disaster relief due to epidemics, floods, tornadoes, and earthquakes. In addition, volunteer doctors are sent to medically needy areas under the auspices of Aesculapian International, a division of DRF. Aesculapian International is a link between physicians, dentists, and senior medical or dental students from all over the world and the overseas areas where they are desperately needed.

Occupation Information:

From its headquarters in Santa Barbara, Aesculapian International sends doctors and medical instructors to more than twenty-five countries for clinical work, to teach or to temporarily replace local personnel. The Action Overseas Program also serves paramedical personnel and experts in health related fields willing to offer some of their time and skills in these same areas. The program is nondenominational, nongovernmental, and nonpolitical. Doctors for Direct Relief are emissaries who combine overseas travel with visits to hospitals served by DRF. They analyze the program's effectiveness and make suggestions for further improving assistance. Long-term assignments, for at least one year, generally offer transportation and compensation based upon the economy of the location. On short-term assignments of less than one year, traveling expenses are usually paid by the volunteer. Work is done without compensation, but, in many cases, room and board are provided.

Further Information—Write to:

Executive Secretary
Aesculapian International
A Division of Direct Relief Foundation
P.O. Box 1319
Santa Barbara, California 93102

Relevant Bibliography Titles: 34, 42, 61, 63, 67, 69, 70, 72, 73, 80, 83, 102, 103.

DO IT NOW Foundation

Nature and Purpose: The DO IT NOW Foundation is a national nonprofit, charitable, and educational organization involved in providing truthful drug education to young people, adults, and professional people. It's In-School drug education program lasts several weeks and involves equal student/parent/teacher education. The Foundation also publishes a wide variety of anti-drug literature. Their many printed materials for students, teachers, and parents offer the only information generally available from those who have actually used the drugs they are writing about.

Occupation Information: The DO IT NOW Foundation staff includes counselors for persons with drug-related problems. Persons with prior drug experience are preferred in these positions. The In-School drug program utilizes advisers—people who work on in-school education; they are often called upon to go to one part of the country or another to advise or speak at high schools and colleges, or to hold professional and parent seminars. Requirements for these positions vary. There are no salaries for either position.

Further Information—Write to: Director
DO IT NOW Foundation
P.O. Box 3573
Hollywood, California 90028

Relevant Bibliography Titles: 9, 10, 22, 23, 32, 34, 41, 66, 67, 79, 95, 105, 111.

The Thomas A. Dooley Foundation

Nature and Purpose: The Thomas A. Dooley Foundation, founded in 1961, is a nonprofit, nongovernmental, nonsectarian voluntary organization providing technical and material assistance to the developing nations of Asia in the fields of medicine, health education, and community development on a self-help basis. For over a decade doctors, nurses, medical technologists, and volunteers have battled for life and improved health in Vietnam, Laos, India, and Nepal.

In addition to the Foundation's headquarters in San Francisco, there are several committees located in major cities across the United States which give assistance in fund raising and publicity for the Foundation.

Occupation Information:

The major kinds of occupations utilized by the Foundation can be broken into two distinct groups; one relating to health and medical technical assistance, this comprising physicians, nurses, and technologists who work in training and service roles in the program. The second category is administration and support through maintenance which is designated by country. Because of the training responsibilities inherent in each of the programs abroad, the technical staff are required to have a minimum of two years' practical experience beyond their formal studies. They are expected to demonstrate leadership and teaching capabilities during this time and to be prepared to work at an instructor level in their services abroad. Language requirements are not rigid. Overseas staff are contracted for a minimum period of 18 months with the Foundation providing round-trip transportation, reasonable housing and food on location, and monthly compensations of $300 for physicians and $150 for other health workers. Administrator and maintenance salaries are in accordance with the experience and capabilities of the applicant.

Further Information—Write to:

The Thomas A. Dooley Foundation, Inc.
442 Post Street
San Francisco, California 94102

Relevant Bibliography Titles:

3, 6, 12, 31, 42, 67, 69, 72, 73, 80, 83, 102, 103.

Encampment for Citizenship

Nature and Purpose:

Encampment for Citizenship has been running programs since 1946 when it was founded by Mr. Algernon D. Black and Mrs. Alice K. Pollitzer under the sponsorship of the American Ethical Union and its affiliated societies. Since 1946 over 4,500 young men and women have participated in six-week encampment programs in such places as New York, Puerto Rico, Kentucky, Montana, California, Mexico, and Arizona; many overseas students have participated.

The Encampment is now dedicating its efforts to the education of youth in facing and meeting the distinctive problems of the 1970s and, as in the past, is offering significant opportunities for young people to further their knowledge of other racial, religious, and economic groups while helping clarify the meaning of democracy and informing young adults on how they might help bring about solutions for pressing social problems.

Occupation Information: Each Encampment has distinctive features, and each group of students and staff join in developing their own program. Encampment staff members are highly motivated young teachers, human rights and community organization workers. They must be experienced and well qualified to deal with workshop topics such as ecology, educational reform, human rights, and crime and punishment. A staff orientation session where staff members of all sites meet is held in New York prior to the opening of the sites. Sites vary from year to year. General Staff members receive a salary of $350. Educational Staff members and nurses receive $600. Board, room, and round-trip transportation are provided all staff, in addition to their salaries. Contracts are signed in the spring.

Further Information—Write to: Encampment for Citizenship, Inc.
2 West 64th Street
New York, New York 10023

Relevant Bibliography Titles: 15, 32, 34, 41, 55, 58, 67.

Environmental Defense Fund (EDF)

Nature and Purpose: The Environmental Defense Fund (EDF) came into being as a result of a lawsuit filed on Long Island in 1966, which took the Suffolk County Mosquito Control Commission to court to stop the spraying of DDT. Expert witnesses described the environmental disasters caused by DDT. Although the suit was finally dismissed, the scientific evidence, plus the accompanying publicity, persuaded the county to block any further use of the pesticide. This demonstrated that science and the law could work together successfully to stop polluters.

Incorporated in 1967, EDF serves as a legal action arm for the scientific community. It is a nationwide coalition of scientists, lawyers, and citizens dedicated to the protection of environmental quality through legal action and through education of the public.

The Executive Committee of the Board meets regularly to review cases currently in litigation and to select other offenders to be challenged. Cases are chosen to lessen severe environmental problems and establish useful legal precedents. EDF concentrates on following a few cases to completion rather than diversifying beyond the point of effectiveness.

Occupation Information: EDF's staff is composed almost entirely of attorneys with litigation experience or scientists of the Ph.D. level. Assistant-type positions at EDF are held by men fulfilling their alternative service requirements. They must have interests and backgrounds compatible with the needs of EDF.

Further Information—Write to: Environmental Defense Fund
162 Old Town Road
East Setauket, New York 11733

Relevant Bibliography Titles: 14, 18, 23, 28, 34, 95, 105, 111.

The Eye-Bank for Sight Restoration

Nature and Purpose: Founded in 1944 by Dr. R. Townley Paton and a group of associates, The Eye-Bank for Sight Restoration is recognized as the first center of its kind and has served as an inspiration and guide in the founding of over eighty other eye-banks located throughout this country and abroad.

The primary purpose of The Eye-Bank for Sight Restoration is the collection and distribution of eye tissues, donated upon death, to surgeons whose patients can be benefited by corneal transplants. Over the past twenty-five years The Eye-Bank has: Provided 10,262 blind and partially blind men, women, and children with improved sight. Increased eye donations from a few pairs in 1944 to the present level of more than 1,000 a year; a total of 15,743 eye donations that have almost eliminated the long waiting period for treatment. Provided training for surgeons from all over the world in the techniques of corneal transplantation. Established an Eye Tissue Bank of over 16,000 specimens, the largest and most complete in the world, for use in research.

Occupation Information: The Eye-Bank employs technical and medical personnel. Position titles include: research associate, technician, and nurse. Medical, college or university, and nursing degrees are required as well as previous experience. Salaries are competitive.

Further Information—Write to: The Eye-Bank for Sight Restoration, Inc.
210 East 64th Street
New York, New York 10021

Relevant Bibliography Titles: 21, 32, 34, 57, 79, 110.

Foreign Policy Association (FPA)

Nature and Purpose: The Foreign Policy Association (FPA) was founded over a half century ago, in 1918, by men and women who had joined together to preserve the peace by advocating America's adherence to the League of Nations. They stayed together for the sake of a broader task: developing an informed, thoughtful, and articulate public opinion on major issues of American foreign policy.

FPA is the major private, nonpartisan, educational agency concerned exclusively with citizen understanding of foreign policy. It is primarily concerned with the provision of a wide variety of services in the field of national education regarding U. S. foreign policy issues. Its programs are designed to expose issues and alternative courses of action and to bring under scrutiny the main arguments for and against them.

FPA is governed by a Board of Directors representing widely differing viewpoints and experience in business, education, and other professions. It operates through its national headquarters in New York and regional offices in the East and the West.

Occupation Information: The FPA staff numbers approximately forty, most of whom are in the national office in New York City. Most professional staff members are consultants on the techniques and organization of educational programs concerned with foreign policy issues. Only a few positions are concerned primarily with research, writing, and other substantive phases of international affairs. The nature of FPA's activities is such that they do not require skill in languages; and the Association has no operations abroad.

Further Information—Write to: Assistant to the Director of Personnel
Foreign Policy Association
345 East 46th Street
New York, New York 10017

Relevant Bibliography Titles: 3, 34.

Foster Parents Plan

Nature and Purpose: Foster Parents Plan was founded in 1937 in Spain during the Civil War by John Langdon-Davies, an English correspondent, and another compassionate Englishman, Eric Muggeridge, a travel agent. The two men organized committees in England and the United States to enlist people who would contribute to the support of homeless Spanish children and become their Foster Parents.

Foster Parents Plan, Inc. is an American philanthropic agency engaged in an international program for the care, maintenance, and development of distressed children and their impoverished families. PLAN is a nonsectarian, nonpolitical, and nonendowed organization. The program provides funds and guidance to the needy children and their families who come under PLAN care. Emphasis is placed on the education of the children, but the importance of every individual in the family is considered, as is the family as a whole. Social services are also provided with the aim of preventing the disintegration of families under severe economic distress.

In each country in which Foster Parents Plan operates, Foster Children and their families benefit from the sustained guidance and counseling of social workers, medical and dental care, and a monthly cash grant. Distributions of goods such as vitamins, household and school supplies, and other useful items are part of most programs. Foster Parents Plan's Special Services Fund provides small amounts of money for emergency needs and loans for small businesses.

PLAN is governed by a Board of Directors who determine broad policy and to whom ultimately, all directors and staff are responsible. International Headquarters is in New York City; and PLAN has field headquarters in Hong Kong, Indonesia, Korea, the Philippines, Vietnam, Greece, Bolivia, Brazil, Columbia, Ecuador, and Peru.

The organization, which started in 1937 with one small Spanish boy, now has an enrollment of over 53,000 children in ten countries. More than 110,000 Foster Children representing twenty-nine nationalities have been graduated from PLAN care to financial independence.

Occupation Information: Foster Parents Plan sends Directors and Assistant Directors to its programs abroad. Otherwise, all staff, including social workers, doctors, etc., are nationals of the country in which the program is working.

Field Directors may be required to establish offices, select local staff, and negotiate with government officials. They must study the poverty conditions, educational system, general economic situation, housing and medical provisions, and develop a PLAN program that best meets the needs of these various conditions. Responsibilities include: training and supervising local staff; maintaining the standards and selections of applicants and general standards of operation; fiscal planning and such other planning, organizing, and directing effort as may be needed.

Requirements for this position include administrative experience in overseas work, preferably in the area of welfare or related fields; and the ability to organize, train, direct, and supervise the PLAN program. Field Directors undergo a training program at a functioning PLAN office abroad. Starting salary is $12,500 per year.

Assistant Directors perform similar functions; less previous experience is required; and their salary is $8,000 per year plus housing.

Further Information—Write to: Foster Parents Plan, Inc.
352 Park Avenue South
New York, New York 10010

Relevant Bibliography Titles: 6, 11, 12, 27, 29, 30, 34, 41, 42, 61, 67, 69, 73, 80.

Foundation for Cooperative Housing (FCH)

Nature and Purpose: The Foundation for Cooperative Housing was established in 1950 to promote the development of cooperative housing. Its founders believed that the co-op approach could contribute significantly to meeting the need for better housing at lower cost for

43

all income groups, including low and moderate income families.

The Foundation, whose trustees serve without pay, has been given a nonprofit, tax-exempt status. As a result, it has benefited from several foundation grants and contracts to conduct intern training programs and pursue various experimental or research housing projects.

Since its inception, the Foundation has sponsored approximately 45,000 units of housing throughout the country. Technical assistance is furnished to developing co-ops through the Foundation's three wholly-owned subsidiaries: FCH Services, FCH International, and TechniCoop, Inc. Housing cooperatives have experienced rapid growth due to the achievements of their members and development efforts of the Foundation. Through FCH Services, Inc., the Foundation provides the expertise needed to bring together all the elements of a successful cooperative community. FCH represents the prospective home owner from the time the land is first located for development until after the housing project is completed and members have assumed occupancy.

FCH never profits from the land or buildings of cooperatives it sponsors; it represents the consumers—the prospective cooperative members.

Occupation Information:	Many FCH positions call for technical knowledge of one or several aspects of housing as required by ongoing programs. Employees in these positions are classified as Housing Development Specialists. They assist in the development of low and moderate income cooperative, nonprofit sales or rental, limited dividend, and rural housing projects. Requirements include a bachelor's degree or equivalent practical experience in related fields. Salaries are competitive.
Further Information—Write to:	Personnel Director Foundation for Cooperative Housing 1012 14th Street, N.W. Washington, D.C. 20005
Relevant Bibliography Titles:	9, 13, 34, 68, 95.

Friends of the Earth (FOE)

Nature and Purpose: Friends of the Earth (FOE) was founded July, 1969, by David Brower. It is a membership organization, with a staff that provides leadership and research on environmental campaigns. Principal emphasis is on public policy, which the organization influences through lobbying and through liaison with the executive branch of the federal government.

Occupation Information: FOE has no specific position classifications. Staff members in Washington, D.C., work principally in the field of research support for major campaigns, such as those against strip-mining, against stream channelization, for pollution taxes, against the Alaska oil pipeline, and for parks and wilderness in various parts of the country. Staff in the field offices are less specialized, and they work with the press and with other citizen groups. Positions usually require experience in research or environmental leadership. There are no particular educational requirements. Staff members learn by working directly with more experienced staff. There are no salaries.

Further Information:—Write to: Friends of the Earth
620 C Street, S.E.
Washington, D.C. 20003

Relevant Bibliography Titles: 14, 18, 23, 28, 34, 95, 105, 111.

Girl Scouts of the U.S.A.

Nature and Purpose: Girl Scouts of the United States of America, a national voluntary nonprofit corporation, was founded in 1912 and chartered by Congress in 1950.

The Girl Scouts of the U.S.A. offers a continuing informal education program to girls between the ages of seven through seventeen. The Girl Scout program, carried out in small groups with adult volunteer leadership, provides these girls with opportunities to choose values and test them in life experience; to help them make critical decisions; to let them explore life's opportuni-

45

ties. Through a wide range of activities in the arts, the home, and the out-of-doors, girls gain new knowledge and skills which they are encouraged to put to use for the benefit of their families, friends, and communities. Troop activities for all ages reflect the elements that give Girl Scouting its distinctive character: adherence to the ethical code embodied in the Girl Scout Promise and Laws; troop management; service; citizenship; international friendship; and health and safety.

The national organization directs and coordinates the Girl Scout movement in the United States; charters local councils, which are independent nonprofit corporations financed by voluntary public givings. There are more than 450 Girl Scout councils providing the Girl Scout program in all fifty states.

The Girl Scout organization has a membership of three million girls and 2/3 million adults who work as volunteers. About 2,500 professional staff members are employed locally and nationally.

Occupation Information: There are a vast number of paid executive positions in Girl Scouting. Positions on the national level, either at headquarters in New York or in the six National Branch offices, are so highly specialized that they require proven experience in any one of the following fields: general administration, adult education, public relations, personnel, community relations, fund raising, finance, publishing, retailing, data processing, and other fields. Opportunities exist to work in socially or economically deprived areas. Many staff members start in councils using leadership skills working with adult Girl Scout volunteers and other community leaders. In addition to positions on the council and national level there are staff positions in Europe and the Far East to help the volunteers serve girls, mostly at U.S. military bases. These positions, requiring a high degree of independent action and responsibility, require at least three years minimum Girl Scout experience.

Requirements for a position vary depending upon the job itself. A candidate's experience, both paid and volunteer, her personal attitudes, education, and general skills are evaluated in terms of the requirements of a particular position. Previous Girl Scout experience is *not* required except as noted above. Salaries vary from $6,000 to $20,000 but are competitive within the area.

A wide range of career opportunities exist for those who like to work with people. Anyone who has previously worked with youth and community volunteers, who has served in inner-city and poverty areas, or who has knowledge of finance, public relations, personnel, administration, and camping experience, can put these skills to work.

46

Further Information—Write to: Girl Scouts of the U.S.A.
Recruitment & Referral Division
Personnel Department
830 Third Avenue
New York, New York 10022

Relevant Bibliography Titles: 15, 27, 34, 41, 55, 58, 67, 77, 112.

Goodwill Industries of America

Nature and Purpose: The first Goodwill Industries was started in Boston in 1902 by Dr. E. J. Helms, a clergyman, who applied practical religion to a humanitarian need. There are now over 145 units dotting the entire map of the United States and a number representing the movement in foreign countries.

Goodwill Industries are nonprofit, locally autonomous agencies organized to provide rehabilitation services, training, employment, placement in industry, and opportunity for personal growth as an interim step in the rehabilitation process for the handicapped, disabled, and the disadvantaged. Through the professional application of recognized techniques of rehabilitation as well as proven procedures developed through continuing research, the organizations seek to assist those needing services to attain the fullest development of which they are capable, regardless of religion or ethnic origin. The selling of articles reconditioned, assembled, or made by such persons as part of their vocational rehabilitation is included in the program.

Because the basic workshop program of a Goodwill Industries is an industrial-type operation and produces a large percentage of earned income in relationship to its operating costs, it has many characteristics of a business, but since its purpose is to serve people, it is essentially a health and social welfare organization.

Goodwill Industries of America, Inc., is the national organization of which the local units are voluntary members. Governed by a Board of Directors, it provides a variety of services to the local units—national leadership, stature and recognition, program counsel, recruitment and training of executives, public relations materials, workshops and conferences, legal and legislative assistance, accreditation, publications, records, and reports.

47

Occupation Information: Each Goodwill Industries is headed by an Executive Director and governed by a Board of Directors. The Executive, working with the Board, formulates and gains approval of the program, plans and directs the work of the staff engaged in its execution, enlists and maintains community participation, represents Goodwill Industries in civic activities, initiates and directs research and special studies, recruits and trains volunteers, and participates in fund raising activities. Requirements for this position include a college degree and some technical or management experience. Candidates are sent to one of several Goodwill Industries serving as training centers where they intern for either a six-month or two-year period, depending on their background and training needs. A tuition grant is paid during the training period. When all the requirements have been met, candidates are awarded a certificate and are nominated to a board of directors for placement.

Local Goodwill Industries also employ personnel to staff the major divisons of work. Titles and brief descriptions of some of these positions follow:

Director of Personnel Management and Rehabilitation—Administers the areas of activities relating to employees and clients, their jobs, employment benefits, discipline, social life, rehabilitation, physical well-being, and general morale.

Operations Director—Directs the activities of all production departments, salvage operations, and building operation and maintenance.

Public Relations Director—Directs a well-rounded public relations program including all forms of publicity, promotion, campaigns, and areas relating to the Goodwill image necessary to gain public support.

In addition to the positions described, career opportunities are available in the following areas: Counseling; Occupational Therapy; Physical Therapy; Nursing; Social Work; Psychology; Psychiatry; Chaplaincy; and Workshop Supervision. These staff, professional, technical, and industrial-type positions require education and experience in specialized fields.

Salaries, for all positions, vary from city to city, depending upon size of city, community and Goodwill Industries resources, experience and qualifications of applicant, and degree of responsibility to be assumed.

Further Information—Write to: Director of Educational Resources
Goodwill Industries of America, Inc.
9200 Wisconsin Avenue, N.W.
Washington, D.C.20014

Relevant Bibliography Titles: 32, 33, 34, 41, 55, 65, 67, 77.

Guiding Eyes for the Blind

Nature and Purpose: Guiding Eyes for the Blind is a national service incorporated in the State of New York with its principal area of service being the United States and its territorial possessions. The primary purpose of this voluntary, nonprofit organization is to provide independent mobility via guide dogs to those visually handicapped individuals who are physically, mentally, and emotionally prepared to benefit from it.

The work of the agency's Breeding Division is an essential element in providing the best unit possible through the breeding and development of the most suitable dogs for guide dog work. In the Training School a staff of professionally trained instructors conducts a prescribed 26-day course designed to teach capable visually handicapped persons the techniques and procedures necessary to properly utilize the services of a well-trained guide dog.

In its comparatively brief sixteen-year history, Guiding Eyes for the Blind has graduated approximately 1,200 units—dog and master—and currently has units operating in over forty states and Puerto Rico.

Occupation Information: Most of the Guiding Eyes for the Blind training staff have had some prior background with either blind people or animals. Academic requirements are flexible, but a minimum of a high school education is required, and many on the staff have an advanced education in subjects which relate to the work. Prerequisites needed in a guide dog instructor include the ability to work effectively with a dog; empathy and the ability to communicate effectively with a blind person. There are relatively few people who possess enough patience and understanding to work effectively in this field. Also, due to the nature of guide dog instruction, long hours and weekends are often required while students are in class.

Further Information—Write to: Guiding Eyes for the Blind, Inc.
106 East 41st Street.
New York, New York 10017

Relevant Bibliography Titles: 21, 30, 32, 34, 67.

Health Research Group

Nature and Purpose:

The Health Research Group is a Washington-based consumer-oriented group conducting studies in three general areas: food and drug/product safety (Food and Drug Administration); occupational health and safety; and the health care delivery system.

Activities involved in such studies might include the following:

FDA: (a) Analysis of FDA structure and function with respect to new drug applications and removal of products. This involves gaining familiarity with relevant medical literature and federal regulations and interviewing of government officials. And (b) Responding to acute problems arising from need to remove dangerous food, drugs, and products from the market.

Occupational Health and Safety: (a) Familiarity with Occupational Safety and Health laws and the roles of the Department of Health, Education, and Welfare and the Department of Labor. (b) Reviewing literature regarding one or two specialized occupational hazards in response to requests from local unions for help in working through occupational health problems. And (c) Site visits to meet and discuss with workers the information about occupational hazards in their working places.

Occupation Information:

The Health Research Group offers two types of fellowships to qualified persons who can undertake the areas of research discussed above. The first, a three-month fellowship, is primarily aimed at students who can spend a summer with the group or who have electives during the year allowing them to take time off. A limited number of subsistence fellowships (up to $600 depending on the financial needs of the student) are available. The second type of fellowship is for a full year. A subsistence salary of $4,500–$7,000 is offered, depending on professional experience. Although students can apply for this full-year program, the Health Research Group prefers applications from postgraduate M.D.'s or other health personnel.

50

Further Information—Write to: Health Research Group
1025 15th Street, N.W.
Suite 601
Washington, D.C. 20005

Relevant Bibliography Titles: 14, 23, 34, 41, 51, 105, 111.

Inter-American Development Bank

Nature and Purpose: The Inter-American Development Bank, established on December 30, 1959, is a regional agency with a membership of twenty-four nations of the hemisphere, including twenty-two Latin American countries, the United States and Canada. The Bank's operations are dedicated to the promotion of the economic and social development of Latin America. To date the Bank has invested $4.7 billion in loans to promote this development. These resources are helping to finance projects valued at about $14 billion in such economic and social fields as agriculture and industry; electric power, transportation, and communications; water supply and housing; higher, technical and vocational education; preinvestment studies, export financing, and tourism.

The Bank also provides technical assistance in these fields to stimulate project preparation and planning at the national and regional levels, to create and strengthen development institutions, and to insure the adequate execution of the projects financed.

In line with its functions and the evolving needs of its member countries, the Bank in the 1970s anticipates a substantial intensification of its lending and technical assistance activities, particularly for projects fostering rural and urban employment opportunities, development of technical personnel and skilled labor, and expansion of nontraditional exports.

Occupation Information: Requirements for lending and technical assistance positions with the Bank include adequate education and/or experience in the developing banking field and, quite frequently, a thorough knowledge of two or more of the Bank's languages, which are English, Spanish, Portuguese, and French. Personnel are assigned for the most part at the Bank headquarters in Washington, D.C., but also in Latin America. Salaries are similar to those of other international organizations.

51

Further Information—Write to: Personnel Office
Inter-American Development Bank
808 17th Street, N.W.
Washington, D.C. 20577

Relevant Bibliography Titles: 3, 6, 11, 12, 17, 61, 63, 83, 112.

International Bank for Reconstruction and Development (IBRD)

Nature and Purpose: The World Bank, known officially as the International Bank for Reconstruction and Development, is the largest and oldest international organization providing development finance to the developing nations of the world. It was founded at the United Nations Monetary and Financial Conference held at Bretton Woods, New Hampshire, in July, 1944, and began operations in 1946.

The World Bank Group comprises four organizations—the Bank itself, the International Development Association (IDA), and the International Finance Corporation (IFC), all of which are associated with the United Nations as Specialized Agencies, and share the task of providing and encouraging investment to raise levels of production and standards of living in the less developed countries; and the International Center for Settlement of Investment Disputes (ICSID), the organization which deals with disputes between governments and foreign investors.

The Bank does not confine its activities to lending; it also provides a wide variety of technical assistance. The Bank assists developing countries in evaluating projects, in appraising the needs and potential of particular economic sectors, in drawing up national programs of economic development or in carrying out other development tasks. A variety of training programs are also provided. Both the Bank and IDA finance the expansion of basic services like transportation, electric power, communications, and water supply, and both also finance industrial, agricultural, and educational projects. IFC assists private ventures through equity investments and loans by entering into underwriting and standby agreements in support of security issues and encouraging the participation of other investors.

Occupation Information: The World Bank, together with its affiliates, offers qualified young men and women a wide range of careers in economic development. The staff of the World Bank Group of Institutions includes specialists of many kinds: engineers, economists, lawyers, agronomists, administrators, educators, and others. The total staff, including professional and nonprofessionals, numbers about 2,400 from 79 countries. Most of the Bank's staff are stationed in Washington, but the Bank has a few offices or missions in other countries. There is no nationality quota system in selecting and promoting Bank Group personnel. Nevertheless, subject to the paramount importance of securing the highest standards of ability and of technical competence, due regard is paid to recruiting personnel on as wide a geographical basis as possible. The equivalent of a master's degree (as defined in the United States) in a field related to the work of the Bank Group is the minimum academic requirement. Entrance salary rates are determined by academic qualifications and experience.

Further Information—Write to: Personnel Division
International Bank for Reconstruction and Development
1818 H Street, N.W.
Washington, D.C. 20433

Relevant Bibliography Titles: 3, 11, 12, 83, 102, 103, 112.

International Development Foundation (IDF)

Nature and Purpose: The International Development Foundation (IDF) was incorporated in the State of New York in April, 1961, as a nonprofit membership corporation. Legal recognition has been granted in all countries in which it operates. Substantial Latin American programming began in July, 1962.

IDF seeks in its programs, in the developing countries in Latin America, to add community organization to the development process, so that the human resources of the community itself may be added to the inventory of assets available for promoting change. While a number of factors are required to achieve self-sustaining development—natural resources, capital, and technology are three prime examples—IDF seeks out those situations in which other requisites are available, and then strengthens the community organizations and leadership without which progress might not occur, despite the presence of economic advantages.

The Foundation's programs are an effort to create functional, two-way links between the people and their national leaders; between economic self-interest at the base level and economic plans and assistance programs initiated by governments; between the desire of free citizens to share power and the need of the State to obtain their constructive participation.

While the initial thrust of IDF activities is broadly aimed at bringing middle and upper level national leadership into direct contact with their natural constituency, through mutual participation in training projects, it is also the aim of the Foundation that this training lead to the formation of independent new popular institutions which promote civic and economic development in rural areas. In particular, IDF has concentrated on the formation of the following: village civic associations; rural marketing cooperatives and their regional federations; and labor unions of landless rural workers.

Occupation Information: At IDF, management skills are measured not only by how well programs are administered, but also by how effectively American staff members are able to work with the host-country personnel who must administer development projects long after the Foundation's departure. In view of IDF's specialization in Latin America, fluent Spanish is a basic requirement for all IDF Representatives, as is an appreciative understanding of the social customs and cultural values of the area. A degree in one of the social sciences and prior experience in Latin America are required.

Further Information—Write to: International Development Foundation, Inc.
205 East 42nd Street
New York, New York 10017

Relevant Bibliography Titles: 3, 6, 11, 12, 34, 53, 61, 63, 73, 83, 102, 103.

International Executive Service Corps (IESC)

Nature and Purpose: The International Executive Service Corps (IESC) was organized in 1964 by a group of American businessmen to help speed economic growth and strengthen private enterprise in the developing countries. IESC is a business-to-business operation. It is a nonprofit corporation that sends seasoned volunteer business executives on short-term assignments abroad to counsel companies which have requested assistance on management problems. In operation since January, 1965, IESC has approved requests for assistance from about 2,700 enterprises in 46 countries. Its volunteer executives have helped improve food production and health standards, textile and apparel manufacture, investment and banking practices, construction methods and transportation systems, industrial processes, merchandising and marketing programs, mining and natural resource development, government and educational services, communications and tourist facilities. Their knowledge of modern managerial practices has been shared with businesses of all sizes.

Occupation Information: IESC recruits experienced executives to volunteer for short-term assignments abroad, usually only three months at a time. Most are recently retired; others are still active in business and are made available by their U.S. companies. While travel and living expenses are paid for the executive, and for his wife if she accompanies him, he serves without other compensation. In some cases, the assignments may be extended by mutual consent, or a later follow-up mission may be planned.

Further Information—Write to: Director of Executive Selection
IESC
545 Madison Avenue
New York, New York 10022

Relevant Bibliography Titles: 2, 34, 42, 53, 59, 61, 69, 73, 83, 102, 103.

International Legal Center (ILC)

Nature and Purpose: The International Legal Center (ILC) was established in late 1966 as a nongovernmental, nonprofit organization with headquarters in New York City. The primary objective of the ILC is to cooperate with the developing countries in their efforts to reform legal education, to improve the competence of the legal profession, and to strengthen legal institutions within the general framework of each country's legal system, tradition, and contemporary needs.

Among the activities of the ILC specifically directed to the achievement of these aims is a program of Overseas Service

Fellowships which enables recent U.S. law school graduates to work in governmental, academic, and other institutions in developing countries as a means of acquiring practical knowledge of the host country's legal system and problems, thus helping to strengthen the competence of U.S. lawyers in the field of law and development in relation to Africa, Asia, and Latin America.

Occupation Information: Each fellowship post, offered by the ILC to a recent law school graduate, is identified by an ILC representative in conjunction with responsible persons in the host country. Depending on the availability of such positions, up to ten awards are made each year. The duration of the assignments is generally twenty-two to twenty-four months. The stipend offered is $7,200 per annum, plus various allowances connected with overseas service. International travel of a Fellow and his dependents is also included.

Further Information—Write to: International Legal Center
866 United Nations Plaza
New York, New York 10017

Relevant Bibliography Titles: 3, 11, 34, 53, 63, 73, 87, 112.

International Social Service, American Branch

Nature and Purpose: International Social Service, American Branch, is the American Branch of International Social Service (ISS) a worldwide nonsectarian organization headquartered in Geneva, Swtizerland, with branches or cooperating agencies in more than a hundred countries. Organized in 1921, the International Social Service, American Branch, makes it possible for United States caseworkers and counselors to help the individual or family with a problem which crosses national boundaries. It also provides the same help to Americans overseas and to foreign nationals who may need social services in the United States.

Services provided include: Planning the placement of children with American families including children already known to the parents; assistance to individuals and courts in settling the guardianship of children; service such as postplacement supervision and the securing of paternal releases to facilitate an adoption plan; counseling on marriage problems, the adoption of stepchildren, survivors' rights; confirmation of social history information on behalf of American couples living outside the United States who are seeking to adopt children; assisting with immigration, repatriation, deportation problems, and planning family reunions including the migration of related children; counseling to motivate the responsible person to support spouse and children; social services to United States patients abroad and their families here as well as assistance in evaluating the social aspects of treatment requests from abroad; counseling for unmarried parents who are abroad, planning for U.S. children born out of wedlock outside the United States, seeking acknowledgment of paternity; and assistance in obtaining documents, locating individuals, and material assistance.

Occupation Information: International Social Service, American Branch, employs both trained social workers and administrative personnel. There is only one office in the United States, and all volunteer and full-time employees work there. On-the-job training is an important part of the program, because ISS is dealing with very technical and complex immigration and legal matters. Educational requirements are commensurate with the responsibilities of each position.

Further Information—Write to: International Social Service
American Branch
345 East 46th Street
New York, New York 10017

Relevant Bibliography Titles: 3, 10, 29, 32, 34, 41, 67, 112.

International Voluntary Services (IVS)

Nature and Purpose: International Voluntary Services (IVS) was chartered under the laws of the District of Columbia in 1953. It was organized by a group of people committed to the idea that volunteers could make an important contribution by establishing person-to-person contacts with people of another country.

IVS is a private, nonprofit organization which has been engaged in development projects overseas at the "grass roots" or "people to people" level. Primary emphasis centers around the general fields of education, agriculture, and rural development. Volunteers come primarily from America but ivs is interested in increasing its multinational representation at all levels of its organization. No project is begun until it has been carefully thought through and fully discussed with the inhabitants of the area where it will be implemented. The local people must want, approve of, and agree to actively participate in any project in which ivs volunteers work.

Ivs volunteers work in the field broadly defined as community development. This includes one or a combination of the following types of activity: general agriculture; agricultural credit; poultry and animal husbandry; plant experiment; propagation and distribution; range management; reforestation; irrigation; well drilling; low-cost housing; sanitation and village improvement generally. They also serve as elementary and secondary school teachers, with the great majority as English language, vocational, and science teachers.

Occupation Information: Ivs recruits carefully selected young men and women willing to learn a foreign language, prepared if necessary to live in remote villages and to work directly with local people. If they are engaged in teaching or in youth or student activities, they may live in provincial towns or in principal cities, but in any case they live simply and without ostentation. Most ivs personnel are recent college graduates with training in a field that relates to rural development, education, and social work in the broadest sense of the term. A college degree is not required if the applicant is competent in a certain needed skill such as nursing, farming, mechanics, or youth leadership. Team members are sought who have skills, training, and experience that enable them to be helpful to people in a wide range of activity affecting their welfare. In many ivs projects, farm background is a key asset in providing such help. In educational work, farm background is not a prerequisite, and ivs seeks recruits with liberal arts backgrounds and teaching experience. Ivs personnel are offered a two-year contract, under which they are obligated to follow the guidance of ivs and its administrative staff. They are guaranteed all necessary expenses plus a cash salary of $80 per month.

Further Information—Write to: International Voluntary Services, Inc.
1555 Connecticut Avenue, N.W.
Washington, D.C. 20036

Relevant Bibliography Titles: 3, 6, 31, 46, 48, 51, 53, 59, 60, 63, 73, 80, 83, 90, 102, 103.

IRI Research Institute (IRI)

Nature and Purpose: IRI Research Institute is a privately established, nonprofit, membership corporation of the State of New York. IRI is engaged in applied agriculture and environmental research and development, primarily in tropical and subtropical regions. The Institute has had over twenty-one years of technical experience in Latin America.

IRI's charter permits it to operate anywhere in the world. The headquarters are in New York and the field staff includes experienced senior professionals, competent technicians, and other employees. Scientific and practical technical contributions are published from time to time as bulletins or technical notes.

The Institute, both alone and with other groups, has focused its efforts on programs designed to improve food production. Their activities may be divided into three main categories: IRI provides technical services in agricultural research, development, and extension to help indigenous research and extension agencies improve their capabilities; using funds from private grants, foundations, and government organizations, IRI has long conducted its own research on specific problems of economic importance; and increasingly, IRI has been involved in training and education to impart skills and attitudes regarding agricultural research, extension, and development.

Occupation Information: IRI offers career opportunities to Ph.D. level personnel in the soil, plant, and animal sciences for persons with sufficient practical field experience. Most contracts are written for periods of two years subject to renewal according to the terms of the particular contract with the sponsoring international organizations, such as FAO and the World Bank. Personnel are required to be already trained with sufficient field background experience. Assignments are in tropical and subtropical overseas locations. Salaries are commensurate with experience.

Further Information—Write to: IRI Research Institute, Inc.
One Rockefeller Plaza, Room 1401
New York, New York 10020

Relevant Bibliography Titles: 6, 12, 61, 63, 73, 102, 103.

Joint Action in Community Service (JACS)

Nature and Purpose: JACS—Joint Action in Community Service—is a nonprofit agency formed to help young people who leave Job Corps training adjust to a new job and to help them become useful, productive citizens.

The formation of JACS, in 1967, was initiated by leaders of national Protestant, Catholic, and Jewish agencies involved in the war on poverty. Its Board of Directors represents a wide range of business, labor, educational, and service organizations as well.

Working on the local level through churches, service clubs, and other community organizations, JACS enlists volunteers to meet and help Job Corps young people on their return to community life. The idea is to help a young person make the most of his new chance in life, a chance that he has earned from months of hard work and study.

JACS headquarters is located in Washington, D.C., but coordination of community volunteer forces is done through seven regional offices.

Occupation Information: The JACS national staff is employed in either an administrative or secretarial capacity. It is their responsibility to recruit, train, and coordinate the activities of the more than 5,000 JACS volunteers throughout the country. The JACS volunteer in the local community helps direct a Job Corpsman to employment channels that will best utilize his new skills and training.

Further Information—Write to: Joint Action in Community Service
1730 M Street, N.W.
Washington, D.C. 20036

Relevant Bibliography Titles: 31, 32, 34, 41, 59, 62, 67.

Just One Break (J.O.B.)

Nature and Purpose: Just One Break is a nonprofit, privately operated agency. Its aim is to find full-time employment for the physically handicapped. J.O.B. meets three vital needs in the community: it provides the disabled employee with a job suited to his capabilities and interests; it provides the employer with workers whose background and experience fulfill his job requirements; and it helps assure a fuller utilization of human resources and skills. No fees are charged; and since it was founded in 1949, J.O.B. has placed more than 10,000 handicapped people.

Occupation Information: Applicants are referred to J.O.B. from several sources. They are required to have a medical prior to an interview. Once the medical information is received, the applicant is given an appointment for an in-depth interview and evaluation of skills by a placement interviewer. Upon the completion of the evaluation, the interviewer then tries to match the skills or potentials of the applicant with jobs that are available. In addition, active recruitment of new companies is continually pursued by J.O.B.'s placement interviewers.

Further Information—Write to: Just One Break, Inc.
373 Park Avenue South
New York, New York 10016

Relevant Bibliography Titles: 9, 21, 32, 33, 34, 41, 67.

Robert F. Kennedy Memorial

Nature and Purpose: The Robert F. Kennedy Fellows Program is a living memorial to the late senator. A primary objective of the Memorial is to offer constructive outlets for the moral, intellectual, and physical energies of young people. The Fellows Program is a tangible means of recognizing, challenging, and reinforcing both individuals and organizations seeking social justice and attacking the causes of poverty and discrimination.

Work in the Fellows Program is presently focused on the *rights of children*. Overall, the Memorial is concerned that all children have the right to enough food to insure normal growth, decent shelter, good preventive and corrective medical care, a good education, and protection against aggravated physical and mental abuse.

The Memorial is focusing on three concerns: (1) *Educational rights of Indian children*—Efforts are focused on developing independent schools controlled by Indians and modifying county

61

and federal school policies affecting Indian children. (2) *Rights of dependent and delinquent children*—Fellows investigate the power and administration of public guardianship over children who are wards of the state. (3) *Educational rights of Chicano children*—This involves community work to change unjust policies in school systems with large numbers of Chicano children.

Occupation Information:

Fellows are placed with local, regional, or national private or public "host" organizations having strong commitment to one of the three areas mentioned above. Placements are not principally to provide training for Fellows (although, obviously, this will occur) but to assist host organizations in their work. Organizations are considered for placement of Fellows only if they are prepared to work for basic social change. Fellows receive a base salary of $5,000 per year. In some cases, this salary may be supplemented by a host organization. Fellow assignments of not less than one year are made at the following intervals: October, January-February, May-June.

Further Information—Write to:

The Robert F. Kennedy Memorial
c/o The Fellows Program
1054 31st Street, N.W.
Washington, D.C. 20007

Relevant Bibliography Titles:

1, 13, 14, 15, 27, 31, 46, 51, 55, 59, 62, 104.

Lutheran World Relief

Nature and Purpose:

Lutheran World Relief was established on October 11, 1945, in New York as a direct response to need in Europe following the war. In 1971 Lutheran World Relief had program involvement in Korea, Taiwan, Hong Kong, Vietnam, India, Tanzania, Zambia, Ethiopia, Cameroun, Nigeria, Jordan, Israel, Brazil, and made shipments, especially of medical supplies, to a number of other countries. Programs are in the field of social service with special stress on material assistance, but with a rapidly developing involvement in development projects.

Occupation Information:

Lutheran World Relief employs administrators, technicians, doctors, nurses, social workers, agriculturalists, community development workers, and physiotherapists. For service in Vietnam, learning the Vietnamese language is required. For service in Cameroun, French is a requirement. A college degree or its equivalent plus some experience is required. Overseas assignments are for two or three years. Assignments may be in Asia, Africa, the Middle East, or Latin America. Language training is provided for Vietnam service. Modest salaries are supplemented with housing and utilities.

Further Information—Write to: Lutheran World Relief, Inc.
315 Park Avenue South
New York, New York 10010

Relevant Bibliography Titles: 2, 6, 29, 31, 41, 42, 52, 53, 59, 60, 61, 69, 70, 72, 73, 80, 83, 100, 102, 103.

MEDICO (a service of CARE)

Nature and Purpose: MEDICO (Medical International Cooperation Organization) was founded in 1958 by Dr. Peter D. Comanduras, now a member of its Advisory Board, and the late Dr. Thomas Dooley, to act as "physicians to the world." It merged with CARE (Cooperative for American Relief Everywhere) in 1962.

MEDICO, a nongovernmental, nonsectarian, nonprofit service of CARE, Inc., offers health education and services to underprivileged areas of the world where there is a serious deficit in and an urgent need for medical care and health protection. Without regard to race, religion, or political persuasion, MEDICO offers qualified physicians, dentists, nurses, and technicians an opportunity to serve in their professions overseas.

MEDICO programs are instituted at the request of the host governmental authorities, under agreements whereby the host provides such facilities, services, equipment, supplies, and professional and student personnel as lie within its capability. MEDICO in turn provides physicians, dentists, and paramedical personnel who work with host personnel in the development of the country's own health program. MEDICO's programs are cooperative and are planned to lead to local self-sufficiency.

In a typical year MEDICO, working with host professional personnel, helps half a million diseased or maimed persons, whether it be assistance at childbirth, performance of major surgery, combating of malnutrition, or teaching simple home hygiene. While

63

serving, MEDICO personnel are also teaching both local medical counterparts and patients—the former in methods of modern medicine; the latter in sanitation, hygiene, and nutrition.

Occupation Information: The MEDICO program is designed to incorporate fully trained medical personnel only. They must be graduates of a professional school and have proper degrees and licensing. The following groups undertake MEDICO's work overseas:

Long-Term MEDICO Teams—Qualified physicians, nurses, technicians, and physical therapists serve overseas for two years on modest salaries plus living allowances. They must have at least one year of postgraduate professional experience and a significant part of their training must have been undertaken in the United States or Canada.

Volunteer Specialists—Augmenting the work of these MEDICO teams are groups of volunteer specialists, internists and surgeons in all the various specialties, nursing instructors, and hospital administrators. Coming from all parts of the United States and Canada, they spend a month each in programmed areas on a rotating basis. They pay their own air fare and living expenses.

Further Information—Write to: Leonard J. Coppold, Director
MEDICO Long-Term Personnel
660 First Avenue
New York, New York 10016

K. L. Hastings, Maj. Gen., USA, Ret.
Director, MEDICO Volunteer Personnel
2007 Eye Street, N.W.
Washington, D.C. 20006

Relevant Bibliography Titles: 3, 6, 12, 31, 34, 42, 67, 69, 72, 73, 80, 83, 102, 103.

Migrant Legal Action Program

Nature and Purpose: The Migrant Legal Action Program was established in August of 1970 as a successor to the legal staff of the Migrant Research Project. Subject to future grant restrictions or special requirements imposed by the Office of Economic Opportunity, the program has operated and expects to continue to operate along the following lines: prepare and collect litigation papers relating to administrative and court litigation in all areas of migrants' concern, and periodically distribute this information as well as analyses on pending and recently adopted legislation and other legal administrative developments; cooperate with programs serving the needs of migrant and rural populations when they request representation of Washington counsel, or request assistance in obtaining information from or presenting materials to administrative agencies and congressional committees; furnish technical assistance to administrative agencies and congressional committees on matters affecting migrant needs and concerns; in selected areas, upon appropriate referral, the agency will engage in litigation as co-counsel or in an "of counsel" capacity; stand ready to provide telephone advice and other technical assistance to any program or individual in need of legal advice or the assistance of a Washington representative; and continue to provide training to persons serving the needs of migrants and other rural poor, including assistance to summer law student programs and personnel of OEO-funded migrant organizations.

Occupation Information: The Migrant Legal Action Program is staffed by attorneys and law clerks; most have prior experience in serving the needs of migrant and seasonal farm workers. The work itself is in the area of poverty law dealing with migrants and seasonal farm workers. The requirements for the various positions consist of interest, willingness to learn when experience is lacking, willingness to put in long and strenuous hours, and past experience or schooling in poverty law. Knowledge of the Spanish language and culture is helpful, although the program provides some training in that area. Salaries are dependent upon knowledge and skill, as well as what monies are available at any given time.

Further Information—Write to: Migrant Legal Action Program, Inc.
1820 Massachusetts Avenue, N.W.
Washington, D.C. 20036

Relevant Bibliography Titles: 1, 8, 14, 24, 25, 62, 90, 94, 98, 104.

Muscular Dystrophy Associations of America (MDAA)

Nature and Purpose:

Muscular Dystrophy Associations of America (MDAA) was founded in 1950. It is a national voluntary health organization, and is dedicated to the scientific conquest of muscular dystrophy and related neuro-muscular diseases.

MDAA supports an international program of research grants related to the diseases of the neuro-muscular unit. MDAA also supports the Institute for Muscle Disease, a major research center in New York City which began operations in 1959.

The Association renders a wide variety of direct services to patients through its 325 affiliated chapters and through a nation-wide network of clinics. In addition, MDAA conducts educational programs for both the general public and members of the medical profession.

Occupation Information:

The following are beginning career positions in MDAA:

District Directors—are responsible for the implementation of the policies and program of the Association within an assigned territory.

Program Directors—assist District Directors in advancing the Association's local program.

Patient Service Coordinators—locate and help patients; and assist in providing patient services.

A college degree or previous work experience is required for these positions. On-the-job training and guidance is provided by experienced personnel. Salaries vary depending on the position and location of the assignment.

Further Information—Write to:

Muscular Dystrophy Associations of America, Inc.
1790 Broadway
New York, New York 10019

Relevant Bibliography Titles:

4, 9, 22, 31, 41, 57, 67, 77, 79.

NAACP Legal Defense and Educational Fund (LDF)

Nature and Purpose:

The NAACP Legal Defense and Educational Fund was established in 1939 by the National Association for the Advancement of Colored People. It has since become separate and distinct from the founding organization. LDF (Legal Defense Fund), as it has come to be known, has its own Board of Directors, its own policies, staff, and budget. Although it has pursued its own route, it retains the founding initials in its name as a reminder of its heritage and as a mark of identity which distinguishes it from numerous other "legal defense funds" which have come into being.

The multifaceted program of the LDF is designed to further the rule of law in the United States by making the promise of equal justice under law a reality for all Americans. Through creative use of the law, the Legal Defense Fund has pioneered social progress during its thirty-three years. It continues to operate on the frontiers of the law in areas affecting our daily lives: employment, education, housing, urban renewal and land use, municipal facilities, consumer fraud, prison reform, and the administration of justice. Its current docket is over 700 cases—the largest legal load of any public service organization. LDF's Division of Legal Information and Community Service is engaged in broad local problems, North and South, to inform citizens concerning their rights, to monitor and report on the use of funds voted by Congress for specific purposes, and to open new avenues of employment for people whose jobs have become obsolete because of modern technology. Its National Office for the Rights of the Indigent protects the poor, regardless of race, color, or creed, from injustices inflicted upon them because of their poverty.

The Legal Defense Fund also operates a Legal Training Program, to correct the critical shortage of black lawyers in the United States, now but one percent of the American bar.

Occupation Information:

LDF has regular staff attorneys and intern attorneys. The interns work with LDF for one year after completing law school. This serves to give them a wide range of experience. Once the internship is completed these attorneys are assigned by LDF to various parts of the country to serve where they are most needed in addition to functioning as cooperating attorneys for the Legal Defense Fund. Salaries are competitive.

67

Further Information—Write to: NAACP Legal Defense and Educational Fund, Inc.
10 Columbus Circle
New York, New York 10019

Relevant Bibliography Titles: 1, 8, 10, 14, 24, 25, 94, 98.

National Council on Crime and Delinquency (NCCD)

Nature and Purpose: The National Council on Crime and Delinquency, formed in 1907, is the only national, nonprofit, private agency working to prevent and control crime and delinquency by tapping both professional expertise and citizen action. NCCD is not a direct service agency but works to improve the operation of agencies which are doing direct service. It has pioneered in setting standards and promoting model legislation to upgrade treatment services, personnel, and even the physical design of criminal justice facilities.

NCCD operates out of a New York City headquarters, four regional offices, twenty state offices, and a national research center in Davis, California. The Research Center conducts original research on the nation's criminal justice system and provides services and consultation to other agencies. An Information Center located in New York City collects, summarizes, stores, and distributes the latest data on crime and delinquency from all over the world. It circulates this information to key professionals in the criminal justice system and allied fields. NCCD sets standards for the criminal justice system with the help of its expert advisory councils. Each meets regularly to deal with specific problems in their areas of expertise. NCCD's legal staff and its Council of Judges create guidelines and model legislation. These "legal blueprints" are circulated to judges, trial lawyers, police, prosecutors, and legislators. At the state and local level, NCCD's field staff work to see that these acts and guidelines are put into effect. Through its Survey Services unit in New York City, NCCD conducts surveys of public agencies ranging from a juvenile court to the entire correctional system of a state.

Occupation Information: NCCD's large professional staff is composed of nearly one hundred specialists in a variety of fields including: law, court services, penology, prevention, probation, parole, detention, research, community organization, and organized crime. Many of these positions are classified as consultant, researcher, and community organizer. As a national standard-setting agency, NCCD requires a minimum of a master's degree and three years of employment in a criminal justice agency. An educational background in the social sciences is also required. Salaries are competitive.

Further Information—Write to: National Council on Crime and Delinquency
Paramus, New Jersey 07652

Relevant Bibliography Titles: 9, 19, 24, 34, 56, 77.

National Easter Seal Society for Crippled Children and Adults

Nature and Purpose: The National Easter Seal Society, organized in 1921, is the pioneering health agency actively concerned with the care and welfare of crippled children and adults. The National Easter Seal Society for Crippled Children and Adults (better known as the National Easter Seal Society) acts as a central service organization for fifty state societies, the District of Columbia and the Puerto Rican Society. The National Society designs and acquires Easter Seals and supplies for distribution and maintains a staff of specialists in the areas of management and organization, education, care and treatment of the handicapped, fund raising, and accounting, who provide consultation to affiliates.

Easter Seal facilities nationwide encompass a wide range of direct services for handicapped children and adults. Specialized treatment of the disabled is given through some 3,000 programs of more than 2,000 state and local affiliates in the fifty states, the District of Columbia, and Puerto Rico. Services are adapted to specific community needs and are given through rehabilitation and treatment centers.

Occupation Information: The Society operates a *Personnel Registry*—a comprehensive personnel service in the rehabilitation field. Registrants with varied backgrounds in rehabilitation are referred to career positions with Easter Seal affiliates. Positions in rehabilitation and treatment centers include the following professional categories:

Physical Therapist—uses the therapeutic properties of exercise, heat, cold, electricity, ultra-sound, and massage to help a

69

patient develop his physical potential to the fullest extent; teaches a patient how to use crutches or an artificial limb to perform everyday functions and to live within the limits of his capabilities.

Occupational Therapist—uses purposeful activity as treatment for individuals with physical or emotional disabilities.

Speech Pathologist—diagnoses and plans therapy for children and adults whose speech is impaired.

Audiologist—is concerned with the problems and disorders of human communication caused by hearing abnormalities.

Special Education Teacher—helps provide the handicapped child with the opportunity to learn—despite a physical, communicative, or learning disability or emotional disorder.

Rehabilitation Counselor—is concerned with helping a handicapped person choose, prepare for, and find useful employment in the occupation for which he is best suited.

Medical Social Worker—is responsible for a patient's welfare both during and after his treatment. He is concerned with the special demands and pressures which can affect a patient, socially, economically, and psychologically.

Recreation Therapist—provides a complete year-round calendar of events to promote the social, physical, mental, emotional, and spiritual growth of the handicapped.

Rehabilitation Nurse—is the member of the rehabilitation team who executes the plan of patient care on a 24-hour basis; and is in constant contact with the client.

Psychologist—uses his specialized knowledge of human behavior to learn about a patient's abilities, interests, and emotional state; he may provide psychotherapy to help the client arrive at an understanding of his disabilities and adjust to living in society.

Further Information—Write to: The National Easter Seal Society for Crippled Children and Adults
2023 West Ogden Avenue
Chicago, Illinois 60612

Relevant Bibliography Titles: 9, 10, 21, 22, 23, 30, 31, 32, 33, 41, 55, 57, 65, 67, 77, 79, 110.

National Foundation—March of Dimes

Nature and Purpose: This voluntary health agency was founded in 1938 by the late President Franklin D. Roosevelt as the National Foundation for Infantile Paralysis. In providing funds which made possible both the Salk and Sabin vaccines, the Foundation became the first voluntary health agency to conquer an epidemic disease that had caused worldwide crippling and death throughout the history of man. With the conquest of polio, the organization in 1958 changed its name to the present form and expanded its program to include birth defects. The National Foundation now supports nationwide programs of research, medical service, and public and professional education seeking to prevent birth defects.

Occupation Information: The majority of career positions with The National Foundation fall into two categories: Field Representatives and Executive Directors.

The National Foundation employs one or more Field Representatives in every state of the union depending on population. He is the link between National Headquarters and the local Chapter and the volunteers associated with that Chapter. He assists volunteers in creating and expanding local programs in the area of birth defects prevention and treatment. In addition, he cooperates with them to inform the public of the research and other medical programs supported by The National Foundation. A major part of the Field Representative's responsibility is to enlist volunteers and guide them in conducting the March of Dimes fund raising program each January to finance national and local programs.

The Executive Director is a staff position existing in major metropolitan areas. This Executive is responsible for carrying out National Foundation programs and fund raising campaigns on the local level in close cooperation with volunteer workers from the communities included within his Chapter area.

There is a great deal of flexibility concerning requirements for these positions. In general, however, the National Foundation seeks college graduates who have majored in the arts, journalism, or social studies. The salary scale on the basis of longevity and degree of responsibility ranges from approximately $7,000 to $18,000 per annum.

Further Information—Write to: The National Foundation—March of Dimes
1275 Mamaroneck Avenue
White Plains, New York 10605

Relevant Bibliography Titles: 4, 9, 32, 41, 57, 67, 77, 79, 95, 110.

National League for Nursing (NLN)

Nature and Purpose: The National League for Nursing is a membership organization which was formed in 1952 to improve nursing, and thereby health services, through a coalition of community leaders, nurses, allied professionals, nursing service agencies, and schools of nursing. NLN fosters community planning for nursing as a primary component of comprehensive health care, the development of nursing manpower, and high standards of nursing service and education.

NLN's headquarters are in New York City. There are branch offices in San Francisco and in Atlanta. Forty-four constituent leagues for nursing implement national programs at the community level. These leagues are organized on city, state, or area bases. Many have local action groups to stimulate community interest in and cooperative planning for nursing and comprehensive health services.

Major services of NLN include: consultation; accrediting nursing education programs; professional testing services; surveys and publications; and acting as a central source of information on trends in nursing, personnel needs, community nursing services, schools of nursing, and governmental programs affecting nursing services and education.

Occupation Information: The League has an experienced staff of consultants who travel throughout the country. Most of the positions require background and experience in nursing education and administration. Many positions require a master's degree; several require a doctorate. Most of NLN's consultants are based in New York. The League also has a group of consultants who work with constituent leagues. With the exception of one in the south and two in the west, they work out of the New York office. These consultants need background and experience in community organizing rather than nursing education specifically. Salaries vary with the responsibilities of each position.

72

Further Information—Write to: Director of Personnel
National League for Nursing, Inc.
10 Columbus Circle
New York, New York 10019

Relevant Bibliography Titles: 22, 32, 41, 57, 67, 68, 77, 110.

National Tuberculosis and Respiratory Disease Association (NTRDA)

Nature and Purpose: The National Tuberculosis and Respiratory Disease Association (NTRDA), a national organization linking state and local groups, was founded in 1904. NTRDA has constituent associations in every state, most of which have local associations affiliated with them. NTRDA supports research projects; engages in educational campaigns to control respiratory diseases; and seeks to stimulate, spearhead, and support community action against tuberculosis and other respiratory diseases.

Occupation Information: Local and state associations throughout the country offer career opportunities in several areas of work. Brief descriptions of relevant positions follow:

The Executive Director is in charge of a state or local TB-RD association, working under the volunteer Board of Directors. He heads the team, administers the budget, supervises the staff—and takes the lead in working in the community, planning and organizing health programs and services with government agencies and other groups.

A Program Consultant or Field Representative usually works for a state association to guide and assist locals, or on the national staff as consultant to states. Or he may serve in an area where there is no local, helping a volunteer committee or operating on his own in small communities.

Program Associate is the title applied to the professional staff member doing general community organization work.

The Fund Raising Director manages the Christmas Seal Campaign and other approved fund raising methods.

Most positions require from two to five years' previous experience. Salaries in the TB-RD associations depend on the size of the organization and the level of the job. A beginner may start at about $7,000 or more.

73

Further Information—Write to: Chief, Recruitment and Training Unit
National Tuberculosis and Respiratory Disease Association
1740 Broadway
New York, New York 10019

Relevant Bibliography Titles: 4, 32, 41, 57, 67, 77, 79, 110.

The Nature Conservancy

Nature and Purpose: The forerunner organization of The Nature Conservancy began in 1917 when the Ecological Society established a Committee for the Preservation of Natural Areas. This society of scientists founded this organization upon the realization that natural lands were rapidly vanishing. In 1950 the Ecologists Union became the Nature Conservancy. The Conservancy, organized for educational and scientific purposes, was recognized as a nonprofit organization in that same year. Today the Nature Conservancy is a private, nonprofit, membership organization devoted to preservation of ecologically and environmentally significant land. Holdings include forests, prairies, swamps, islands, and seashores. The organization has been instrumental in preserving some one-quarter million acres comprised of over 600 projects in almost every state. The Conservancy is the only environmental organization whose resources are solely devoted to preservation of land.

Occupation Information: The Conservancy has a professional staff in the National Headquarters in Arlington, Virginia, and in the Regional Offices in Cincinnati, Minneapolis, and San Francisco. Because The Conservancy relies upon the public for financial support and is a land acquisition organization, the activities of the staff members vary greatly. Within the National Office there are nine functional areas which are concerned with separate aspects of acquiring, preserving, and funding projects. The functional areas include Public Relations, Finance, Membership, Administration, Preserve Management, Legal, Operations (land acquisition), and Development (fund raising). The staff requirements within each area range from professional—requiring B.A. or M.A. in such fields as economics, forestry, law, real estate, and business—to nonprofessional. The salary paid employees varies with the position and is determined by the individual's skills and experience.

Further Information—Write to: Director of Administration
The Nature Conservancy
1800 North Kent Street, Suite 800
Arlington, Virginia 22209

Relevant Bibliography Titles: 14, 18, 28, 34, 105, 111.

Near East College Association

Nature and Purpose: The Near East College Association is the central service organization for six nonsectarian, private American sponsored colleges overseas which bring an opportunity for preparatory and higher education in Greece, Turkey, and Lebanon to some 10,000 students of more than sixty national and cultural backgrounds. During the past century these colleges introduced contemporary education and American principles and practices to the area and have been a significant factor in the development of this important region. Although the colleges are the result of the best efforts of private American philanthropy, they are known and respected as indigenous institutions which operate within the framework of local educational law, preparing men and women for useful careers in their own countries.

Teaching at these schools offers a challenging opportunity for experience in living and working with people of varied cultures through both faculty and student relationships. Americans form only part of the faculty membership and the local staff represents the leaders of the educational and intellectual life of the community.

Occupation Information: Overseas administrators prefer teachers seasoned in classroom procedures and in the actual subject or field to be taught. At the secondary level a bachelor's degree is acceptable for some positions but the majority require a master's. At university and college levels practically all of the positions require a Ph.D., teaching experience, research, and in some instances scholarly publication. It is not necessary for a teacher to know the local language since in all classes taught by Americans, teaching is in English. The usual term of teaching is three years. Salaries depend on experience and educational background.

75

Further Information—Write to: Personnel Services
Near East College Association
305 East 45th Street
New York, New York 10017

Relevant Bibliography Titles: 6, 43, 87, 88, 93.

Near East Foundation (NEF)

Nature and Purpose: Incorporated in 1930, the Near East Foundation is America's oldest philanthropic, nonsectarian, nonpolitical agency devoted exclusively to programs of technical assistance and rural development in emerging nations. Its object is to assist governments of newly developing nations to launch programs of rural and community improvement that, as rapidly as possible, become the full responsibility of that government in matters of operation, financing, and personnel

NEF enters a country only at the invitation of the local government when it has agreed to participate in and support the program in its own country. NEF's major contribution is in the form of experienced technicians who, through modern methods, are demonstrating to host governments and their people how to develop their natural and human resources. This may include emphases like: demonstrations of improved agricultural practices, introduction of new crops, sanitation, disease prevention and control, home and family welfare, rural schools, agricultural and credit cooperatives, animal husbandry, horticulture, and literacy.

Occupation Information: At present NEF has technicians stationed in twelve countries of the Middle East and Africa. Almost all of the Foundation's staff are professionally trained agriculturalists. NEF generally requires five to seven years of successful experience in addition to one or two professional degrees. Tours of duty are for two years. Compensation varies according to qualifications but in general NEF tries to remain competitive with other positions in the agriculture field.

Further Information—Write to: Near East Foundation
54 East 64th Street
New York, New York 10021

Relevant Bibliography Titles: 2, 3, 6, 7, 11, 12, 55, 69, 73, 83, 90, 102, 103.

Opportunities Industrialization Center (OIC)

Nature and Purpose:
Opportunities Industrialization Center was created in 1964 by Dr. Leon Sullivan, a Negro, to provide job training to disadvantaged Philadelphia black people and to give them a chance for a variety of industrial jobs which had long been beyond their reach.

The Philadelphia Opportunities Industrialization Center provides job training service to unemployed and underemployed persons, a motivational and attitudinal service to both the individual and the community, a job placement service to industry, and an on-going prototype, and motivational service to other OICs. Some thirty courses are offered at OIC's five branches located throughout the city. The job training courses range from welding to typing, from brick masonry to plumbing, electronics, air conditioning, sheet metal fabrication, machine shop, and others.

Since the beginning of the OIC program in Philadelphia, over 17,000 people have been trained and close to 12,000 placed in almost every type of job imaginable. OIC trained people range from cooks to computer operators, from welders to women working as secretaries, clerks, and typists.

An OIC national structure has developed from the increasing demands by other cities to have the OIC concept transferred to their locality. As of 1970 there were 39 other OIC cities with a program in some stage of development for a total of ninety OIC affiliates. OIC, conceived s a means of helping Philadelphia's disadvantaged blacks, draws neither a geographical nor a color line today. Some 80 percent of the trainees in San Jose, California, are Mexican-Americans. Sixty percent of those in Roanoke, Virginia, are white.

Occupation Information:
Key staff members in OIC manpower education are the Recruiter, Counselor, Instructor, and J.D. (Job Developer). The ideal OIC staff member should have a liberal arts college degree, a year of study in his specialty and after that, at least three years of experience on a job that is related to his OIC responsibilities.

Recruiters—canvass inner city communities and try to persuade residents to attend the OIC program. This is the only position where education is not a vital prerequisite. The ability to relate to the target people is more important.

Counselors—help the recruit convert himself into a trainee and continue to advise him as he moves through his training cycle.

77

Instructors—are the core of the training itself, and should have "positive" attitudes, teaching techniques, and knowledge of their subjects.

Job Developers—secure commitments from employers to hire OIC-trained personnel; and seek to develop new job opportunities.

Further Information—Write to: Opportunities Industrialization Center, Inc.
1225 North Broad Street
Philadelphia, Pennsylvania 19121

Relevant Bibliography Titles: 1, 8, 13, 25, 31, 62, 74, 94.

Pan American Health Organization (PAHO)/ Pan American Sanitary Bureau Regional Office of the World Health Organization

Nature and Purpose: The Pan American Sanitary Bureau in 1947 became the operating arm of the Pan American Health Organization. Two years later the Bureau also became the World Health Organization's Regional Office for the Americas. The Bureau's foundation in 1902 makes it the world's oldest existing international health organization. It is charged with coordinating international public health work in the Americas. Like WHO itself, it is not a supranational health authority but it is at the service of national health administrations to help them improve the health of their peoples. In addition to its Washington Headquarters, the Bureau maintains zone offices in Mexico City, Lima, Caracas, Buenos Aires, Rio de Janeiro, and Guatemala City.

After almost seven decades of work, PAHO's functions and duties have expanded into four main lines: The control or eradication of communicable diseases, strengthening of national and local health services, education and training, and research. To help the Governments of the Americas in these fields, PAHO provides expert advice and technical assistance, acting also as a clearing house for scientific information and a central coordinating agency.

Occupation Information: The regular staff of the Bureau numbers 1,191, representing fifty nationalities. Of this total, 894 are assigned to Zone Offices and field projects, and 297 are stationed in Washington. Technical health assistance is primarily accomplished by personnel sent to individual countries for periods ranging from a few months to a few years. For this purpose, the Organization seeks the services of highly qualified personnel available for short or long term assignments. Medical officers, nurses, sanitary engineers, entomologists, bacteriologists, and serologists, and health educators are employed for these field assignments.

Medical officers are needed as advisers to governments on broad health programs or as professors in schools and institutes. Other medical staff lead teams to train local personnel in techniques for combating specific public health problems. Nurses are needed as advisers to governments, in the development of public health nursing services or educational programs. Nursing instructors are required, in nursing education teams or as individual teachers. Public health nurses may work individually or as members of field demonstration programs. Other technicians serve as individual instructors in schools or institutes, or as members of teams, in which they are responsible for instruction and demonstration in their special fields. All professional technical personnel should have some training and experience in public health services.

In the administrative field, career opportunities exist for professional positions at the Washington headquarters and Zone Offices located in Latin America. For this type of work, specialized experience is sought in the following: Budget and Finance, Auditing, Administrative Management, Personnel Management, Medical Supplies, General Office Services, Public Information, Editorial, Translation and Reference Services, and General Administration. Salaries for medical officers and sanitary engineers start at about $13,578 per annum; for nursing positions, the base pay ranges from $11,283 to $13,578 per annum. The other types of technical personnel generally are appointed at $9,274 to $11,-283 per annum. Starting salaries for administrative personnel range between $7,258 and $13,578.

Further Information—Write to: Chief, Personnel Section
Pan American Sanitary Bureau
Regional Office of the World Health Organization
525 23rd Street, N.W.
Washington, D.C. 20037

Relevant Bibliography Titles: 6, 11, 12, 53, 54, 61, 72, 73, 87, 88, 112.

Pennsylvania Prison Society

Nature and Purpose:

The Pennsylvania Prison Society, founded in 1787, is the oldest prison reform organization in the country; it has always been involved in direct service to individual offenders and general reform.

Occupation Information:

Positions, pertinent to the functions of the Society, and their specific requirements fall within the following areas: social casework; sociological surveys and analyses; public education; and experimental innovative programs. On-the-job training is provided new staff members. Salaries are competitive.

Further Information—Write to:

The Pennsylvania Prison Society
311 South Juniper Street
Philadelphia, Pennsylvania 19107

Relevant Bibliography Titles:

1, 14, 19, 24, 56, 67, 95.

People, Incorporated

Nature and Purpose:

People, Incorporated is a national voluntary service organization whose original sponsors were: HUMANITAS, Paul Goodman, Paul Krassner, Dick Gregory, and Joseph Heller. At present People, Incorporated runs "free" schools for "difficult brats, or for kids who don't learn so good in the socialist school system." They also have a few spots for people who want to do nitty gritty beginning work on stable farm communities. They do not play encounter, do-your-own-thing games with the work—but otherwise, after work is done staff members can play at what they want. They also don't play Peace Corps, "send me your round pegs only" games.

Essentially, People, Incorporated is a group of people who have dedicated some part or all of their lives to working with kids. They try to live communally with unsprayed foods, lots of woods and grass (green stuff), quiet, and clean air. The kids who are sent to them have been labeled emotionally disturbed—some are— some aren't—but it does require a lot of patience and a high tolerance for dirt, noise, and bad language.

Occupation Information: There are no particular qualifications required for joining People, Incorporated, except a willingness to work, be clean, and live with the kids. People, Incorporated, presently have on staff those who have completed high school on up to those who have Ph.D.'s. Volunteers are given room and board, essential goods, and services, $7.50 a week for riotous living, and all the work they can stand. Volunteers are accepted for as little as three months.

Further Information—Write to: George von Hilsheimer
People, Incorporated
P.O. Box 606
Orange City, Florida 32763

Relevant Bibliography Titles: 46, 48, 59, 104, 105, 111.

The People-to-People Health Foundation / Project HOPE

Nature and Purpose: Project HOPE (Health Opportunity for People Everywhere) is the principal activity of The People-to-People Health Foundation, an independent, nonprofit corporation. Staffed by United States medical personnel, HOPE participates in the development of emerging nations, elevating health standards through health career training programs, and by promoting international friendship and understanding. Using the educational experience gained from service abroad, HOPE's domestic program works with U.S. minority groups.

Project HOPE began in 1958 when President Eisenhower asked William B. Walsh, M.D., a Washington, D.C., heart specialist, to consider initiation of a nongovernment health program to help the people of developing nations. Dr. Walsh's subsequent plan called for refitting a mothballed Navy hospital ship to use as a floating medical center. The U.S.S. *Consolation* was refitted and rechristened the S.S. *Hope*. Her maiden voyage took place in 1960.

The essence of HOPE's programs is education on a people-to-people basis. Skills and techniques are brought to the people and health professionals at home and abroad in their own environment. Programs are adapted specifically to their needs and to their way of life. Operating on the principle of helping people

81

who wish to help themselves, HOPE only goes where it is invited. Invitations come from foreign governments, local medical communities, institutions for medical education, and local civic leaders. Comprehensive programs are developed with local health personnel on a counterpart basis. Persons trained by HOPE are selected from the country in which the *Hope* is serving. Those employed have backgrounds for training others in the medical fields. Local participation is required.

A HOPE mission overseas begins with preplanning by advance medical and paramedical teams which are sent to the host country. A full team of physicians, nurses, and paramedical personnel arrive aboard the hospital ship for a period of ten months. After the departure of the ship, a permanent group of medical and paramedical personnel remain to develop the land-based program.

Preplanning is also the key to a HOPE domestic program in the U.S.A. The program is planned and implemented on a partnership basis with the local medical community. The ultimate goal is for local leadership to eventually take over a program once it has been firmly established by the HOPE team.

Occupation Information: In order that Project HOPE can fulfill its domestic and international goals, The People-to-People Health Foundation looks for certain characteristics in its personnel. The primary consideration is professional competence and experience in the area of specialty. Equally important is the ability to adjust to new living and working conditions. A successful international health worker is dedicated, flexible, and has a strong belief in his mission. In all programs HOPE medical and paramedical personnel are continually teaching by exchanging ideas with counterparts and by working with students.

The period of service on the Hospital Ship, S.S. *Hope* must be for the entire voyage—approximately one year. However, special two-month rotating assignments are available for doctors and dentists. Personnel receive salary and maintenance while on the ship.

Assignments at land-based overseas installations are generally for two years though one-year tours of duty may be considered. All personnel are salaried and may receive housing.

Length of service for programs in the U.S.A. must be a minimum of one year. All personnel are salaried.

Further Information—Write to: Project HOPE
The People-To-People Health Foundation, Inc.
2233 Wisconsin Avenue, N.W.
Washington, D.C. 20007

Relevant Bibliography Titles: 4, 6, 59, 60, 63, 69, 72, 73, 87, 93, 102, 103, 110.

Planned Parenthood of New York City (PPNYC)

Nature and Purpose: Planned Parenthood of New York City (PPNYC) was created in the fall of 1966 as the result of the merger of three separate affiliates of the national Planned Parenthood organization. As an affiliate of Planned Parenthood-World Population, the national voluntary family planning organization, Planned Parenthood of New York City is part of an international network of family planning agencies. PPNYC operates under the belief that modern methods of fertility management offer a basic solution to many of the health and welfare problems of families and individuals.

Through a network of state-licensed centers, PPNYC serves nearly 30,000 New Yorkers annually by providing medically prescribed and medically approved fertility management services. The agency serves patients of any race, creed, or income level. English and Spanish are spoken at all centers. Patients are served through Medicaid or pay fees according to their means. Specialized services to adolescents and premarital counseling are available at many PPNYC facilities, and in one of the centers early abortions are provided. Many referrals are made for help with medical and social problems.

Through the Family Planning Information Service, PPNYC furnishes information, counseling, and referrals on family planning, abortion, infertility problems, voluntary sterilization, and related subjects. The Public Information Department of PPNYC develops and conducts citywide publicity and public relations programs to interpret and promote the goals and services of the agency and the values of family planning.

Occupation Information: The major activity of Planned Parenthood of New York City is in the provision of contraceptive and abortion services in their eight clinics. These clinics are staffed by nurses (who are primarily interviewers and counselors), OB/GYN trained physicians, and doctor's assistants, for whom there are no strict educational requirements but who must be intelligent, accepting of individuals from all walks of life, and interested in the field of family planning. Some clinics also have social workers (M.S.W. degree) and nurse-midwives. Staff at all levels are trained by the Resources Center—a technical assistance and education service affiliated with PPNYC.

83

Further Information—Write to: Planned Parenthood of New York City, Inc.
300 Park Avenue South
New York, New York 10010

Relevant Bibliography Titles: 4, 9, 22, 26, 32, 49, 55, 57, 67, 77, 79, 110.

Planned Parenthood-World Population (PP-WP)

Nature and Purpose: The Planned Parenthood Federation of America was established in 1961. Familiarly known as Planned Parenthood-World Population, the Planned Parenthood Federation of America has grown from a single clinic in Brooklyn to a nationwide network of 181 affiliates, with a total of 620 clinics, operating in 350 cities in forty states and the District of Columbia. Through the International Planned Parenthood Federation, of which it is a charter member, Planned Parenthood-World Population helps national family planning organizations in more than one hundred countries around the world.

PP-WP's principal goals are: to help make information and effective means of family planning, including contraception and voluntary abortion and sterilization, available and fully accessible to all; to educate all American parents to the fact that it serves their own family well-being and the common good to limit family size; to stimulate relevant biomedical, socioeconomic, and demographic research; to combat the world population crisis by helping to bring about a population of stable size in an optimum environment in the United States; and to support the efforts of others to achieve these goals in the United States and throughout the world.

In the United States, Planned Parenthood-World Population gives professional guidance to voluntary birth control programs throughout the nation. Six hundred and twenty clinics, with the help of seven regional offices, bring family planning information, education, and medically supervised services to over 400,000 women of varied social and economic backgrounds annually at little or no cost. In addition, the organization conducts social and clinical research, furnishes and directs professional training of medical and health personnel, and assists city, county, and state governments in developing their own family planning programs.

Occupation Information: The job being done in the national office is basically administrative and a degree in Business Administration is a basic prerequisite. Pp-wp refers people who want to work within the organization on the practical levels (i.e. medical and sociological positions) to affiliates who operate the clinics and have actual contact with the general public.

Further Information—Write to: Planned Parenthood-World Population
810 Seventh Avenue
New York, New York 10019

Relevant Bibliography Titles: 4, 9, 22, 26, 32, 49, 55, 57, 67, 77, 79, 110.

Project Concern

Nature and Purpose: Project Concern, founded in 1962, is a non-profit medical relief organization, operating hospitals and clinics in Hong Kong, Mexico, Vietnam, Appalachia (Tennessee), New Mexico, and Rio Grande Valley (Texas). Project Concern's programs are "self-help" in nature—designed to permit the recipients to become self-sufficient; public health oriented making *prevention* the primary medical ambition; and characterized by internationality, independence, and freedom from specific religious, political, or nationalistic ties.

Occupation Information: Project Concern utilizes the services of licensed medical doctors, nurses, dentists, dental hygienists, dental assistants, pharmacists, laboratory and X-ray technicians who work toward self-sufficiency among those without basic health, education, food, and shelter. Salary, and room and board are provided for a year's service.

Further Information—Write to: Project Concern, Inc.
440 West B Street at Columbia
San Diego, California 92101

Relevant Bibliography Titles: 4, 6, 31, 42, 59, 61, 72, 73, 80, 83, 102, 103.

Public Interest Research Group (PIRG)

Nature and Purpose: Ralph Nader's Public Interest Research Group is one of the largest public interest law firms in the country. PIRG projects are in such areas as consumer credit problems, environmental pollution, public access to governmental and other institutions affecting national policy, Food and Drug and FTC regulatory matters, Civil Service reform, property taxation, and income taxation.

The standard corporate law firm works in the courts, administrative agencies, and legislatures. PIRG practices in all of these fora and also in the public forum.

Occupation Information: PIRG is staffed by attorneys and recent law school graduates. The work requires individual attorney initiative and skill in identifying points of access to institutional decision making processes. The work is intellectually and emotionally stimulating to a degree which far outweighs the low monetary compensation available.

Further Information—Write to: Public Interest Research Group
1025 15th Street, N.W.
Washington, D.C. 20005

Relevant Bibliography Titles: 1, 8, 14, 18, 23, 24, 25, 31, 89, 98.

Salvation Army

Nature and Purpose: The Salvation Army, founded in 1865 in England, is an international religious and social service organization. It is organized and operated on a military pattern. In the charter issued in New York State in 1899 The Army is defined as an organization "designed to operate as a religious and charitable corporation." The original and still paramount purpose of The Salvation Army is to lead men and women into proper relationship with God. William Booth, the founder, however, was a realist and he instituted a welfare program that was and is a manifestation and practical application of the dominating spiritual motive of The Salvation Army. Aid is given whenever and wherever the need is apparent, without distinction as to race or creed and without demand for adherence, simulated or real, to the principles of The Army.

The basic unit of Salvation Army service is the corps. Some cities may contain several corps, popularly known in some areas as neighborhood centers. Each corps is headed by a corps officer, and all corps within certain geographical boundaries comprise a division, under the direction of a Divisional Commander. The corps is the community center for a varied program ranging from regular religious services and evangelistic campaigns to family counseling, youth activities, and other general social activity.

With the aid of counseling techniques, medical resources, and psychiatric therapy, The Salvation Army works through its services and institutions to strengthen individuals and families. In cooperation with governments, foundations, and other organizations, it helps to evaluate social problems and to correct, as far as possible, the conditions leading to individual and community problems.

Occupation Information: While Salvation Army operations are supervised by commissioned officers—men and women called to the evangelical Christian ministry within The Salvation Army, qualified men and women are sought for many professional and semiprofessional positions, regardless of religious affiliation. Career opportunities vary according to The Salvation Army program provided in each community—but professional personnel are needed in: day care centers, nursery schools and children's institutions; boys' and girls' clubs; summer camps for children, mothers and children, and senior citizens; maternity hospitals and homes; clinics; emergency lodges for women and children; clubs for members of the armed forces; centers for the rehabilitation of homeless men and alcoholics; neighborhood centers; residences for senior citizens; correctional services programs and many allied social welfare services; family services programs; foster homes programs; and clubs for senior citizens. Career opportunities are available for: caseworkers, counselors; nurses; youth workers; group workers; occupational therapists; psychologists; physicians; psychiatrists; and many others.

Further Information—Write to: The Salvation Army
National Headquarters
120 West 14th Street
New York, New York 10011

Relevant Bibliography Titles: 15, 20, 22, 26, 27, 31, 32, 41, 50, 55, 67, 77, 112.

United Nations Volunteers (UNV)

Nature and Purpose: The United Nations Volunteers programme (UNV) was established on January 1, 1971, by the General Assembly of the United Nations. In accordance with the terms of its mandate, the UNV is governed by the following basic principles: volunteers are recruited on as wide a geographical basis as possible, with emphasis on recruits from developing countries; volunteers will have the technical and personal qualifications required for the development of recipient countries, including ability to transfer skills; and United Nations volunteers will be sent to a country only at the explicit request and with the approval of the government.

The primary purpose of United Nations volunteers is to make a contribution to the development of the recipient country. Volunteers are associated primarily with development projects of the United Nations system, which include United Nations Development Programme-assisted projects, as well as projects of the specialized agencies and organizations.

Occupation Information: To qualify for admission to United Nations Volunteers a man or woman must be over the age of twenty-one, meet the health standards and personal qualifications established by the UNV, and possess the educational and technical background needed for the post for which he has volunteered. The program is intended primarily to encourage the participation of the younger generation in the cause of development. The broad scope of development projects in the United Nations system, which range from agriculture and teacher training to engine repair and city planning, offers a wide choice to able young graduates from universities and technical institutions and to highly skilled artisans. A UNV tour of service is normally for a minimum period of twenty-four months. In the country of assignment, a United Nations volunteer receives a monthly living allowance in local currency to cover all basic needs for food, clothing, and incidental expenses. He is also provided with free living accommodations.

Further Information—Write to: United Nations Volunteers
United Nations
New York, New York 10017

Relevant Bibliography Titles: 3, 6, 11, 12, 31, 34, 52, 53, 59, 60, 63, 73, 83, 102, 103, 112.

United Seamen's Service (USS)

Nature and Purpose:
The United Seamen's Service is a nonprofit membership corporation that was formed in 1942 to promote and foster the welfare of the seamen and other personnel of the Merchant Marine of the United States and of the United Nations, and to provide and maintain clubhouses and other facilities for their use, and recreational, medical, educational, religious, personal, and other services for their benefit. The USS program has been flexible enough to meet the shifting demands of the changing international situation. The agency operates sixteen overseas units, servicing thirty ports.

Occupation Information:
The primary responsibility of overseas field jobs is management of Centers providing a wide range of services for seamen. Community representation, counseling, and communications are important functions of the field representatives who must continually interpret American voluntary concepts in a foreign setting. In troubled areas of the world USS workers go on board ships to give seamen valuable information about such things as danger spots on the water front, recent incidents, national antagonisms, available transportation, and recreation. Uss workers arrange transportation where none is available and set up recreation programs where it is desirable. Whether they operate a club or work on shipboard, USS workers give personal aid and guidance to seamen, since the problem may involve communication with families, illness and hospitalization, advice and counseling, or any of the many welfare needs that are regularly met for their fellow citizens at home.

Further Information—Write to:
United Seamen's Service
17 Battery Place
New York, New York 10004

Relevant Bibliography Titles:
3, 6, 11, 32, 41, 52, 53, 63, 67, 73, 77.

Wilderness Society (TWS)

Nature and Purpose:

The Wilderness Society, formed in 1935, is a national conservation organization incorporated in the District of Columbia to secure the preservation of wilderness; to carry on an educational program concerning the value of wilderness and how it may best be used and preserved in the public interest; to make and encourage scientific studies concerning wilderness; and to mobilize cooperation in resisting the invasion of wilderness. The Wilderness Society's long-time, broad purpose is to increase the knowledge and appreciation of wilderness, wherever found, and to see established enduring policies and programs for its protection and appropriate use.

The Wilderness Society staff of conservationists with backgrounds in many related fields divides its energies among the wilderness review work on regional and national levels, direct assistance to local groups with workshops, consultant services and educational grants, and reaching the American people through use of periodic wilderness reports, magazine articles, and "conservation alerts." Tws also conducts a not-for-profit wilderness trip program featuring an educational experience for its vacation travelers.

Occupation Information:

Tws's staff of conservationists is located in Washington, D.C., and in the regional office in Denver, Colorado. Consultants also reside in other parts of the country and assist in wilderness review or follow-up with state and local conservation groups in their areas. To qualify for this work and for the professional staff work one needs to have experience in conservation organization work or training in natural area administration, or knowledge of ecology-related subjects, but not necessarily a college degree. Salary range is competitive with other nonprofit organizations in Washington and Denver.

Further Information—Write to:

The Wilderness Society
729 15th Street, N.W.
Washington, D.C. 20005

Relevant Bibliography Titles:

14, 18, 28, 34, 105, 111.

World Education

Nature and Purpose: Founded in 1951, World Education is a private, nonprofit, and tax-exempt U. S. institution. It is founded on the belief that effective learning takes place when educational opportunity intersects with vital daily concerns. World Education's focus is functional education for adults. Specifically, they plan, implement, and support literacy programs related to food production and family planning—the fields most crucial to individual and national development. World Education has initiated field studies and programs in twenty countries.

Occupation Information: World Education sends teachers overseas to establish and maintain their literacy and family planning projects. Projects are now underway in five countries: India, Africa, Turkey, Thailand, and South America. A master's degree in adult education or family planning is preferred; knowledge of Spanish, French, or some Asian language is an asset. Assignments are for an indefinite length of time and salaries are competitive.

Further Information—Write to: World Education, Inc.
667 Madison Avenue
New York, New York, 10021

Relevant Bibliography Titles: 2, 3, 6, 11, 42, 52, 53, 61, 69, 73, 83, 87, 88, 93, 102, 103.

PART II

Federal Agencies

General Information on Careers in the Federal Government

The federal government is the nation's leading employer. Practically every occupation in the country's private economy is now represented by a similar occupation in government, and there are other occupations found only in government. All occupations described or mentioned in this section of the *Guide* fall under the civil service merit system. The majority of these positions are in the executive branch—that is, in agencies under the direction of the President, like the Department of Health, Education, and Welfare, the Department of Transportation, the Environmental Protection Agency, and so on.

In order to be considered for employment with federal agencies it is necessary to make formal application through the Civil Service Commission so that an applicant's eligibility may be determined. This may be done at the nearest Federal Job Information Center or Commission office. Upon receiving a rating from the Commission, an applicant is placed on the appropriate register for his or her qualifications. These eligible lists are established as a result of competitive examination; some examinations require a written test and others do not. In an examination not requiring a written test, the applicant is rated primarily on the experience and education shown in the completed application form submitted. Whether the examination is written or not, the applicant with the highest score is placed at the top of the eligible list. Agencies having vacancies for which the applicant qualifies would then be able to consider him for employment.

The Civil Service Commission functions through 65 area offices located in centers of federal population throughout the country. These offices announce and conduct examinations. They also provide, through Federal Job Information Centers, a complete one-stop information service about opportunities in the area as well as in other locations. Addresses of the Federal Job Information Centers and further information can be obtained by writing to: U.S. Civil Service Commission, Civil Service Commission Building, 1900 E Street, N.W., Washington, D.C. 20415.

Most positions in the federal government are subject to the Classification Act. This means that they are classified into grades of the General Schedule (GS) according to the difficulty and responsibility of the duties. A salary range is assigned to each grade. Congress fixes the salary rates for Civil Service employees. In the Federal Salary Reform Act of 1962, Congress declared that federal salary rates shall be comparable with private enterprise rates for the same levels of work. The following portion of the salary schedule, effective January 9, 1972, covers the grade levels of occupations described in this section:

Salary Range (10 step)

GS-2	$ 5,166—$ 6,714		GS-9	$11,046—$14,358
GS-3	5,828— 7,574		GS-10	12,151— 15,796
GS-4	6,544— 8,506		GS-11	13,309— 17,305
GS-5	7,319— 9,515		GS-12	15,866— 20,627
GS-6	8,153— 10,601		GS-13	18,737— 24,362
GS-7	9,053— 11,771		GS-14	21,960— 28,548
GS-8	10,013— 13,019		GS-15	25,583— 33,260

Department of Agriculture (USDA) Extension Service

Nature and Purpose:

The Extension Service, created in 1914, is the educational agency of the Department of Agriculture. It is one of three partners in the Cooperative Extension Service. State governments, through their land-grant universities, and county governments are the other partners. All three share in financing, planning, and conducting Extension's educational programs. The Extension Service staff represents USDA in this activity.

Extension helps the public learn about and apply to everyday activities the latest technology developed through research by the land-grant universities, the Department of Agriculture, and other sources. The major areas included in the educational efforts are:

efficient production and marketing of agricultural products; improved family living, including nutrition; 4-H youth development; and rural development.

Occupation Information: More than 3,000 Extension offices throughout the nation make up a vast facility for extending knowledge. Some 11,000 professional extension workers—area and county agents—work directly with individuals, families, and groups to help them apply the newest proven technology to the everyday problems and opportunities of living and making a living. Recent college graduates, with a degree in agriculture or a related field, are usually employed in a county as an assistant agent. They may do general work or they may specialize in an area such as 4-H Club work, livestock, farm or home management, or rural development. Salaries for these positions vary among states and counties. They are based on qualifications and previous experience. An assistant agent starts at a (national average) salary of $6,900 to $7,600 per year.

At the federal level, agricultural extension specialists provide leadership in the work of the Federal Extension Program through the fields of program leadership, educational research and training, subject-matter specialization, and educational media. They also assist state extension directors, supervisors, and program leaders in planning, developing, and coordinating national, regional, and state extension programs. The fields just mentioned have positions at the GS-12 through 15 levels and require professional experience.

Further Information—Write to: Personnel Development and Management Division
Federal Extension Service
U.S. Department of Agriculture
Washington, D.C. 20250

Relevant Bibliography Titles: 9, 13, 18, 43, 76, 77, 95.

Department of Agriculture (USDA)
Farmer Cooperative Service (FCS)

Nature and Purpose: Formed in 1953, Farmer Cooperative Service provides research, management, and educational assistance to cooperatives to strengthen the economic position of farmers and other rural residents. It works directly with cooperative leaders and federal and state agencies to improve organization, leadership, and operation of cooperatives and to give guidance to further development.

The Service: (1) helps farmers and other rural residents obtain supplies and services at lower cost and to get better prices for products they sell; (2) advises rural residents on developing existing resources through cooperative action to enhance rural living; (3) helps cooperatives improve services and operating efficiency; (4) informs members, directors, employees, and the public on how cooperatives work and benefit their members and their communities; and (5) encourages international cooperative programs. The Service also publishes research and educational materials and issues *News for Farmer Cooperatives*.

Occupation Information:

The staff of FCS includes agricultural economists, educators, organizers, and rural sociologists. They carry on research in cooperative management, financing, and member relations, and they relate these to specific commodities or farm supplies. Staff are assigned to FCS offices in Washington, D.C., except in the case of work for the Agency for International Development which involves technical assistance to cooperatives and government agencies in the development of their cooperative programs. In the United States, staff members travel widely to get the facts, study co-op operations, and help train co-op directors, managers, and employees. Requirements for these positions are a doctor's or master's degree in socal science or related fields.

Further Information—Write to:

Farmer Cooperative Service
U.S. Department of Agriculture
Washington, D.C. 20250

Relevant Bibliography Titles:

3, 6, 9, 13, 76, 77, 95, 96.

Department of Agriculture (USDA)
Food and Nutrition Service (FNS)

Nature and Purpose:

The Food and Nutrition Service was established in 1969. It leads the nation's effort to wipe out hunger and malnutrition. Its Food Stamp and Commodity Distribution Programs help provide food to poor families, both through the regular food marketing system

98

and through a direct distribution system. Its Child Nutrition Programs help to feed children through the National School Lunch Program, School Breakfasts, Special Milk, and other child-feeding activities in preschool centers and summer programs. When hurricanes and other natural disasters strike, resources of all these FNS programs are adapted to aid its victims.

Occupation Information: Members of the FNS staff include management specialists who work with the high finance of planning a program; food marketing specialists experienced in the jobs of getting food from the plants that produce it, on through transportation channels, and delivered to the warehouses from where it will be distributed to schools and needy people in their homes and in institutions; and home economists and food technologists who help state and local school lunch managers get more and better lunches to children in school. Entry level grades for these positions are GS-5 and GS-7. A degree in agriculture, marketing, home economics or related fields is required.

Further Information—Write to: Personnel Division
Food and Nutrition Service
U.S. Department of Agriculture
Washington, D.C. 20250

Relevant Bibliography Titles: 9, 13, 55, 62, 71, 75, 76, 77, 95.

Department of Agriculture (USDA)
Forest Service

Nature and Purpose: The Forest Service, created in 1905, is primarily concerned with protection and development of our natural resources. The Forest Service administers 154 national forests and nineteen national grasslands containing 186 million acres in forty-one states and Puerto Rico. These lands are managed for multiple use and sustained yield of all the renewable natural resources including timber, water, forage, special products, fish and wildlife, natural beauty, and outdoor recreation.

In addition, the Forest Service cooperates with state agencies and private forest owners; to protect the 450 million acres of state and privately owned forests and critical watersheds against fire, insects, and diseases; to encourage better forest practices for

99

multiple use and profit on the 367 million acres of private forest land; to aid in production and distribution of planting stock for forest and shelterbelt planting; to provide technical assistance in utilization and marketing of forest products; and to stimulate proper management of state, county, and community forests.

Occupation Information:

The staff of the Forest Service includes a wide range of occupations. Foresters, who are specialists in managing timber, range, water, recreation, and wildlife resources, carry out the Service's primary responsibilities. Landscape architects design and develop large recreation areas. Range conservationists in the Forest Service are responsible for helping provide nationwide leadership in forest range conservation, development, and utilization. Engineers design, and supervise projects that contribute to the fuller use and enjoyment of the nation's forests. Backing up these staff members are scientific, professional, and technical personnel. Bacteriologists, forest product technologists, research foresters, entomologists, plant pathologists, and men and women representing many other scientific disciplines conduct research into the diverse problems involved in forest management, wood products, diseases, and insect control. A college degree in an appropriate field is required for entry level GS-5 positions.

Further Information—Write to:

Forest Service
U.S. Department of Agriculture
Washington, D.C. 20250

Relevant Bibliography Titles:

9, 18, 23, 28, 76, 77, 95.

Department of Agriculture (USDA)
Soil Conservation Service (SCS)

Nature and Purpose:

Established in 1935, the Soil and Conservation Service develops and carries out a national soil and water conservation program through 3,000 soil and water conservation districts—districts with 2.2 million cooperating landowners and farm operators. This agency also provides USDA leadership for: Watershed protection projects, the Great Plains conservation program, resource conservation and development, income-producing recreation enterprises, river basin investigations, and the National Inventory of Soil and Water Conservation Needs. In addition, SCS administers the federal part of the National Cooperative Soil Survey and

100

makes and coordinates snow surveys for water supply forecasting in the western states. The scs also gives technical help in support of the national agricultural conservation program. In recent years the services of scs specialists have been used more and more by state, county, and local governments, planning and zoning agencies, and other institutions and organizations in rapidly developing areas to insure proper land and water management. These services take the form of assistance to nonfarm groups in such activities as the provision of municipal and industrial water supply, highway construction, housing developments, recreation facilities, school site development, and strip-mine reclamation.

Occupation Information: Scs work is directed by an administrator and staff in Washington, D.C. State offices and a Caribbean office give technical and administrative supervision to about 2,800 local work units where conservation technicians work directly with landowners and operators, other users and developers, and community planning agencies. At the "grass roots" level, where the bulk of the conservation job is being done, the following specialists are found:

Soil Conservationists—help local people in rural and rural-fringe areas prepare conservation development plans for communities and individual operating units to meet local needs; and give on-site technical assistance in carrying out planned conservation improvements.

Range Conservationists—help ranchers and other range users to determine the potential of their land for producing forage from native plant communities for livestock, wildlife, and recreation and prepare conservation plans to improve the condition of their range.

Soil Scientists—collect, and record for publication, information about the soil.

Agronomists—provide technical guidance on agronomic problems to scs employees, and to landowners and operators who are carrying out soil and water conservation programs.

Woodland Conservationists—give technical guidance, training, and other assistance in woodland conservation to scs employees and soil and water conservation district cooperators.

New employees enter the Service at grades GS-5 and GS-7. A college degree with major study in a related area is required.

Further Information—Write to: Director, Personnel Division
Soil Conservation Service
U.S. Department of Agriculture
Washington, D.C. 20250

Relevant Bibliography Titles: 9, 13, 18, 23, 28, 76, 77, 95.

101

Department of Commerce (USDC)
Office of Minority Business Enterprise (OMBE)

Nature and Purpose:

The Office of Minority Business Enterprise was established in 1969. Under the direction of the Secretary of Commerce, OMBE: coordinates plans, programs, and operations of the federal government and state and local governments, to foster the growth of minority business enterprise; mobilizes and stimulates the activities and resources of business and trade associations, universities, foundations, and professional and other private interests involved in aiding minority enterprise; and maintains an information center for compiling and disseminating helpful information on successful (and unsuccessful) minority business ventures, to benefit and guide new developments in minority entrepreneurship.

Agencies and organizations wishing to participate in the minority enterprise program work directly with OMBE. Minority businessmen, on the other hand, generally work with business development organizations—"OMBE Affiliates"—in major cities across the country. OMBE also maintains relationships with federal inter-agency groups known as Minority Business Opportunity Committees (MBOC) in many cities. In addition, using the vehicle of a government-licensed Minority Enterprise Small Business Investment Company (MESBIC), a new program, in which many major corporations have established venture capital subsidiaries oriented towards the financing of minority business firms, was begun in 1970.

Occupation Information:

OMBE has specialists in government coordination, urban and rural programs, business and professions, financial resources, data banks, foundations and universities, and management assistance. Each of these divisions plays an individual and cooperative role in the nationwide program to close the entrepreneurial gap between whites and nonwhites. A college degree in a related area of study is required for entry level positions.

Further Information—Write to:

Office of Minority Business Enterprise
U.S. Department of Commerce
Washington, D.C. 20230

Relevant Bibliography Titles:

8, 9, 13, 76, 81, 95.

102

Department of Health, Education, and Welfare (HEW)
Food and Drug Administration (FDA)

Nature and Purpose: The Food and Drug Administration is the federal agency responsible for enforcing the present Food, Drug, and Cosmetic Act. FDA protects the health of American consumers by insuring that: foods are safe, pure, and wholesome; drugs and therapeutic devices are safe and effective; cosmetics are harmless; and that all these products are honestly and informatively labeled and packaged. The Administration is also empowered to see that: dangerous household products carry adequate warnings for safe use and are properly labeled; and the hazards incident to the use of other types of consumer products are reduced.

FDA has four major functional organizations: The Bureau of Drugs, which carries on administrative, scientific, and enforcement activities relating to drugs and therapeutic devices; the Bureau of Foods and Pesticides, which is responsible for administrative, scientific, advisory, and enforcement activities to insure the purity, safety, and wholesomeness of foods, and compliance with food standards; the Bureau of Veterinary Medicine, which tests products and evaluates for safety and effectiveness new animal drugs and medicated feeds, and carries on advisory, scientific, and enforcement activities to protect consumers of foods derived from animals; and the Bureau of Product Safety, which administers the Federal Hazardous Substances Act and Toy Safety Amendments to insure safety and proper labeling of products used around the home.

Occupation Information: FDA headquarters offices are located at Rockville, Maryland. There are also offices in Washington, D.C., and Beltsville, Maryland. Field activities are carried out by staff located in ten DHEW Regional Offices, nineteen district offices and the National Center for Drug Analysis in St. Louis, Missouri. Career opportunities exist within all of FDA's bureaus and offices. Food and Drug chemists do both analysis and research. They work principally in the field of analytical biochemistry of foods, drugs, cosmetics, pesticides, food additives, color additives, and medicated feeds. Inspectors examine the sanitary conditions, manufacturing process, and labeling of products in food, drug, and cosmetic establishments; they observe the analytical work performed by industry scientists; and make on-the-spot examinations to detect harm-

103

ful or deceptive adulteration or contamination of materials. Medical officers help develop medical policy on the efficacy and safety of drugs; medical devices; and substances found in, or proposed for use in, foods, drugs, cosmetics, and hazardous household products. Microbiologists with FDA perform bacteriological research and analysis on products and raw materials to detect micro-organisms. The entry level for chemists, inspectors, and microbiologists is GS-5; and an appropriate college degree is required. Physicians (Medical Officers) start at the GS-14 level.

Further Information—Write to: Public Health Service
Food and Drug Administration
U.S. Department of Health, Education, and Welfare
Rockville, Maryland 20852

Relevant Bibliography Titles: 9, 23, 71, 76, 77, 79, 95, 99.

Department of Health, Education, and Welfare (HEW)
Office of Education / Teacher Corps

Nature and Purpose: The Teacher Corps was established by the Congress in 1965 and began operating in 1966. It is a nationwide effort to give poor children better educations by helping universities improve the ways they prepare teachers and local schools improve the ways they use teachers. This effort is carried out through Teacher Corps teams which the universities train and the schools employ.

The Teacher Corps gives poverty-area schools, their communities, and nearby universities the chance to work together to plan and operate innovative programs for the training and use of teachers. The heart of each program is its Teacher Corps teams —committed young Americans who have volunteered for two years of service in poverty classrooms. Each team is made up of five to eight inexperienced teacher-interns led by a veteran teacher. The team serves as a unit—about 60 percent of its time in the classrooms, about 20 percent in education projects in the school neighborhood, and about 20 percent in professional study leading to a master's or bachelor's degree and teaching certification. Three-fourths of Teacher Corps teams are in elementary education.

Teacher Corps teams serve in 140 school districts and five

prisons and study in 87 university training centers in thirty-five states, Puerto Rico, and the District of Columbia. About half the school districts are in major cities and half in small towns and rural areas. There are teams in nearly all of the nation's largest cities; in Appalachia and the Ozarks; in migrant communities and on Indian reservations; in Spanish-speaking communities in New York, Florida, the Southwest, and California, and in correctional institutions in Georgia, Connecticut, Illinois, California, and Oregon.

Occupation Information: Some 3,000 men and women—experienced team leaders and interns—are currently working in teams to develop their skills and their understanding of the education of poor children. The team leaders are certified teachers and usually have a master's degree and about five years' experience. About two-thirds of the interns are college graduates (four-fifths of them with liberal arts, business, or science degrees) and the rest have at least two years of college. Education and experience requirements for new applicants to Teacher Corps projects vary, depending on the nature of the project. No previous education courses are required for interns and, in general, education majors are not selected. All applicants must be seeking a career in the education of the disadvantaged. They must possess the maturity needed for self-directed, self-paced study and be capable of empathy with children and adults with differing backgrounds. Team leaders are paid by local school systems at local salary scales. Teacher-interns receive taxable stipends of up to $90 a week plus $15 for each dependent. Assignments are for two years.

Further Information—Write to: Teacher Corps
Washington, D.C. 20202

Relevant Bibliography Titles: 13, 15, 31, 46, 48, 62, 77, 90, 94, 95, 104, 105, 111.

Department of Housing and Urban Development (HUD)

Nature and Purpose: The overall purpose of the Department of Housing and Urban Development (HUD) is to assist in providing for sound development of the nation's communities and metropolitan areas. HUD seeks to make decent homes in a suitable environment available to all Americans—especially those whose incomes are too low for today's real estate prices. HUD also strives to improve the quality of life in the nation's cities and towns and to ensure that future urban growth will be more orderly than it has been in the past.

The Department provides financial and technical assistance through more than seventy action programs to help states, counties, and communities solve urban problems. It encourages private industry to produce housing more efficiently, to build new communities and to insure and finance housing construction.

Occupation Information: HUD headquarters offices are in Washington, D.C.; field operations of the Department are carried out through a series of regional, area, and insuring offices throughout the country. To accomplish its tasks, HUD's staff is comprised of many professions and occupational fields. There are career opportunities for the following specialists:

Urban Planners develop programs and methods to improve planning coordination in metropolitan areas so that cities may grow in orderly ways. They furnish technical assistance to state, local, and regional governments and advise top federal management on new policy directions and possible new legislation.

HUD architects ensure that design and construction features and cost estimates for HUD-assisted projects comply with federal policies and regulations. They provide leadership and advice in upgrading properties and neighborhoods and building more attractive communities.

The Urban Design Specialist coordinates architectural, environmental, and urban planning principles to create more attractive and liveable cities through improved design.

HUD landscape architects help prepare plans and specifications for landscaping and planting around low-rent housing projects and, on larger projects, recommend methods for maintaining structures, sidewalks, and plantings.

HUD Urban Renewal Specialists help local governments plan and accomplish neighborhood facilities projects to bring health, recreation, and social services to low-income families. They aid in developing urban renewal projects to eliminate slums.

Specialists in Metropolitan Development work with communities in planning projects to provide facilities, preserve open space, beautify urban areas, and promote orderly urban growth. These specialists assist applicants for HUD aid and coordinate the technical review of projects.

As the primary liaison between HUD and local authorities, the Housing Management Specialist reviews general management matters and offers suggestions for developing, maintaining, and using HUD-subsidized housing with maximum efficiency.

Model Cities Specialists are HUD representatives and coordinators in cities that participate in comprehensive improvement projects to restore the social and physical values of entire neighborhoods.

Further Information—Write to: Office of Personnel
U.S. Department of Housing and Urban Development
451 7th Street, S.W.
Washington, D.C. 20410

Relevant Bibliography Titles: 13, 71, 76, 77, 94, 95.

Department of the Interior (USDI)
Bureau of Land Management (BLM)

Nature and Purpose: The Bureau of Land Management was established in 1946. It is responsible for approximately 450 million acres of the nation's public lands—an area more than ten times the size of New England. Of this total, approximately 175 million acres are in eleven western states and 285 million acres are in the state of Alaska. BLM also has responsibilities for mineral leasing on submerged lands of the outer continental shelf and on other federal lands managed by other agencies.

As manager of more than half of all federally owned lands, BLM's primary purpose is the wise administration, selective disposition, conservation, and management of the nation's public lands and resources. These resources include the land itself, minerals, forests, range vegetation, recreation, wildlife, and soil and water.

Major programs of the Bureau are: Surveying the public domain; managing, selling, or leasing land for its best use under the Multiple Use Act or other public land laws; maintaining the vast collection of official records on all public land transactions; managing and protecting public ranges and forests; conserving soil and moisture; administering laws that govern mining and mineral leasing on public land, the outer continental shelf, and certain private lands.

Occupation Information: The Bureau organization consists of the headquarters in Washington, D.C., three detached offices having Bureau-wide responsibilities, a basic field organization of state and district offices, and other field offices which perform limited functions. Within the Bureau, areas basic to resource management include forest management, range management, and outdoor recreation. Foresters in the Bureau participate in the formulation of forest management and timber sale plans, timber sale contracts, compilation of basic forest inventory data, fire protection, and other forest protection activities. BLM Range Managers develop range management plans designed to obtain optimum use of the forage consistent with sustained production and proper coordination with other land uses. Recreation specialists administer, supervise, or perform professional work in planning and coordinating the use of land and water resources to assure that sufficient opportunities are available for the creative use of leisure time outdoors and to protect and enhance the quality of the physical environment for the enjoyment and inspiration of people. Recent college graduates are brought into these Bureau positions at grades GS-5 and GS-7.

Further Information—Write to: Bureau of Land Management
U.S. Department of the Interior
Washington, D.C. 20240

Relevant Bibliography Titles: 9, 18, 23, 28, 71, 76, 77, 95.

Department of the Interior (USDI)
Bureau of Outdoor Recreation

Nature and Purpose: The Bureau of Outdoor Recreation provides guidance and assistance for agencies at all levels of government and private interests concerned with outdoor recreation. As the leader in promoting a coordinated effort in outdoor recreation, the Bureau engages in a wide variety of activities. Planning, basic to any organized undertaking, is one of the Bureau's major concerns. The Nationwide Plan for Outdoor Recreation, which takes into account the plans of federal agencies, states, and local groups, assesses the variety, quantity, and quality of recreation resources, project demand, and makes recommendations on a national scale.

The Bureau also participates in specific planning projects with other federal agencies and assists states with their own outdoor recreation plans. These statewide plans provide the basis for state participation in the land and water conservation fund program and assist state and local officials in deciding on actions to be taken to meet their priority needs.

Studies of recreation resources constitute another major part of the Bureau's work. Usually made at the request of the President, the Congress, or the Secretary of the Interior, these studies examine areas with potential for recreation, to determine their suitability for public recreation purposes, and to recommend appropriate development and management. Other studies are made of water development projects and selected river basins to insure that recreation potentials are considered in planning.

Occupation Information:
The headquarters of the Bureau is in Washington, D.C. More than half of the Bureau's work force, however, is assigned to the Bureau's field organization, which consists of six geographic regions, with offices at Seattle, San Francisco, Denver, Ann Arbor, Atlanta, and Philadelphia. In typical assignments, the Bureau's Outdoor Recreation Planners make studies of recreation needs or resources, prepare recommendations on transportation proposals, evaluate federal agency land acquisition programs, review and draft comments on federal agency environmental statements, evaluate Statewide Comprehensive Outdoor Recreation Plans, consult with state officials on their outdoor recreation programs, or evaluate requests for financial assistance through the Land and Water Conservation Fund. Appointments to this position are made at levels from GS-5 through GS-15. A four-year degree or a minimum of three years of specialized work relating to Bureau programs is required.

Further Information—Write to:
Bureau of Outdoor Recreation
U.S. Department of the Interior
Washington, D.C. 20240

Relevant Bibliography Titles:
9, 13, 18, 71, 76, 77, 95.

Department of the Interior (USDI)
National Park Service

Nature and Purpose:
Since its inception in 1916 the National Park Service has been dedicated to the preservation and management of the nation's scenic and historic areas. The programs of the National Park Service are managed with the ultimate goal of instilling an envi-

109

ronmental awareness in the park visitor. Each visitor's park experience provides the link between the environmental resources of the park and man's natural and cultural foundations.

In 1964, the Secretary of the Interior recommended separate management concepts for three different types of areas—natural, historical, and recreational. The National Park Service, which comprises almost 29 million acres, contains over seventy natural areas which preserve for future generations this country's areas of natural beauty and grandeur; more than 165 historical areas which retell the story of the nation's growth; and over thirty recreational areas which provide space for physical recreation, relaxation, and restoration. The Park Service also administers the National Capital Parks in the Washington, D.C., metropolitan area.

Occupation Information: The Service is headquartered in Washington, D.C., has six regional offices, one planning and service center and more than 270 field areas in the United States, Puerto Rico, and the Virgin Islands. More than 6,000 employees form the permanent staff that carries out the missions of the Service. In addition to the administrative, scientific, engineering, and enforcement staff employed in offices or the field, the Forest Service staff includes Park Rangers, Aides, Technicians, and Guides who work in urban, surburban, and rural areas. Park Rangers work on recreation activity planning, conservation programs, park organization, financial management, supervision of other employees, and other activities related to the management of National Park areas. Technicians and Aides are among their support staff. Park Technicians work on fire fighting crews, and with conservation teams working on soil erosion, plant and insect control projects. Aides work on the more basic tasks involved in fire fighting, conservation programs, enforcing the law, and other jobs related to park and recreation area operation. In historical areas, Park Guides give general informational tours to groups of visitors. Aides and Guides usually start at grade GS-2 or GS-3; education and experience requirements vary. Technicians, who start at grade GS-4, need at least two years of experience or two years of related college level studies. Most new Park Rangers are hired at grade GS-7 and a college degree in a related field is required.

Further Information—Write to: National Park Service
U.S. Department of the Interior
18th and C Streets, N.W.
Washington, D.C. 20240

110

Federal Agencies

Relevant Bibliography Titles: 9, 18, 23, 28, 43, 71, 76, 95.

Department of Justice (USDJ)
Bureau of Narcotics and Dangerous Drugs
(BNDD)

Nature and Purpose: The Bureau of Narcotics and Dangerous Drugs (BNDD) was established in 1968 in response to the need for a single agency to deal with the growing problem of drug abuse. The Bureau is responsible for the enforcement of the laws and statutes relating to narcotic drugs, marihuana, depressants, stimulants, and the hallucinogenic drugs. Its objectives are to reach the highest possible sources of supply and to apprehend the greatest quantity of illicit drugs before they reach the street. To achieve its mission, the Bureau has stationed highly trained agents along the the traditional routes of illicit traffic, both in the United States and in foreign countries.

Besides enforcing the laws, the Bureau also regulates the legal trade in narcotic drugs. This entails establishing import, export, and manufacturing quotas for these controlled drugs. Physicians, pharmacists, and other persons responsible for handling, dispensing, or prescribing narcotics and dangerous drugs may be subject to periodic inspections by Bureau representatives. Such supervision of legitimate trade insures an adequate supply of drugs for medicinal purposes and research, and at the same time is instrumental in preventing diversion of drugs into illicit channels.

Another area of responsibility for the Bureau of Narcotics and Dangerous Drugs is drug abuse prevention. As part of its program to make citizens aware of the hazards of narcotics and dangerous drugs, the agency provides factual information through literature, speakers, films, and displays to a variety of organizations, and to the general public. It also works closely with educators, as well as with local, state, and national government agencies, associations, law enforcement officials, and organizations in planning and conducting abuse prevention programs.

The Bureau also conducts research to expand the knowledge of controlled drugs and their effects in terms of pharmacology and other scientific disciplines. The data gained is used to determine current and future problem areas and the impact on enforcement and prevention programs.

111

Occupation Information: Because of the scope of its operations in the United States and in foreign countries, the Bureau employs a great variety of talents and skills, in addition to physicians, pharmacologists, chemists, pharmacists, professional educators, and administrators. Through its Compliance Investigators the Bureau regulates the legal trade in narcotic drugs. The Investigator's job involves daily contact with drug manufacturers, pharmacists, and doctors. They conduct industry audits; work closely with other federal agencies; and testify in court and administrative hearings. Special Agents of BNDD work in a wide range of activities. Enforcement of the registration provisions of the applicable laws brings them into contact with the drug industry at all levels; enforcement of the criminal provisions of these laws may require them to act as undercover agents; and they also participate in public education programs. Investigators are hired at grades GS-5, 7, and 9; agents, at grades GS-7 and 9. A college degree in a related area and experience is required. Special Agents must also meet a strict set of physical requirements.

Further Information—Write to: Coordinator of Recruitment
Bureau of Narcotics and Dangerous Drugs
U.S. Department of Justice
1405 I Street, N.W.
Washington, D.C. 20537

Relevant Bibliography Titles: 9, 23, 32, 76, 95.

Department of Justice (USDJ)
Bureau of Prisons

Nature and Purpose: The Bureau of Prisons consists of thirty-five major institutions providing custody and correctional programs to approximately 21,000 inmates. These inmates constitute about 5 percent of the total offenders confined in the United States. In addition, community treatment centers operated by the Bureau and located primarily in major metropolitan areas provide a supervised environment and transitional programs for selected offenders who are approximately three months away from release. Bureau facilities and institutions are found in thirty-eight locations throughout the United States.

The primary goals of the Bureau of Prisons are (a) to provide a level of inmate supervision, consistent with human dignity, that will protect the community, provide maximum safety for inmates and staff, and carry out the judgments of the U.S. courts, (b) to increase significantly the number of federal offenders achieving successful post-release adjustments, and (c) to increase program alternatives for those offenders who do not require traditional institutional confinement.

Programs provided to inmates of federal institutions range from basic and advanced education and vocational training to behavior modification. To achieve its correctional goals, the Bureau uses innovative learning techniques and provides intensive counseling for inmates. Increasing emphasis is being placed on providing the individual inmate with realistic occupational and social education to ease his transition back into the community. Inmates may avail themselves of on-the-job training and practical work experience in manufacturing plants operated by Federal Prison Industries,(FPI) Inc.

Occupation Information: The Bureau of Prisons carries on a rehabilitative effort for convicted federal offenders. Teachers participate in the development of education programs, with the achievement of results as the prime criterion. The major thrust is toward attainment of at least sixth-grade level of reading, English-language proficiency where lacking, acquisition of employable skills, and High School Equivalency Certification. Another aspect of rehabilitation involves intensive counseling for inmates. Correctional Treatment Specialists perform many of the casework functions which are assigned to social workers. They work in a wide variety of correctional institutions and with many different types of offenders. The work often consists of intra-institutional and community contacts designed to aid in correcting offenders. Requirements for teachers, who enter at grade GS-9, may be met by various combinations of training, experience, and/or accreditation. Correctional Treatment Specialists are hired at grades GS-9, 11, and 12. A college degree with major study in the social sciences, professional experience, and/or graduate study are required.

Further Information—Write to: Personnel Officer
Bureau of Prisons
U.S. Department of Justice
101 Indiana Avenue, N.W.
Washington, D.C. 20537

Relevant Bibliography Titles: 9, 19, 41, 56, 77, 95.

Department of Justice (USDJ)
Community Relations Service (CRS)

Nature and Purpose: The Community Relations Service was established in 1964 to utilize local and national resources to promote positive social change. The primary function of the CRS has been one of helping to conciliate racial conflicts. Since its inception, however, the CRS has worked unceasingly to bring all available public and private resources to bear on the underlying causes of racial tensions and conflict. The CRS not only aids in resolving disputes and difficulties as they erupt, but also helps communities to achieve the kind of progress which will enable them to avoid racial upheavals. Its goal is to help bring about rapid and orderly progress toward securing a life of justice, equal opportunity, and human dignity for all American citizens.

The CRS assists communities either on its own initiative, at the request of state or local officials, or upon inquiry of other interested organizations or persons. This assistance takes many forms: helping communities to identify their social problems that are more apparent from an objective, outside perspective; aiding communities in developing and applying their resources for rapid, orderly social and economic change in minority communities; helping to speed delivery to communities of federal programs and services designed to improve social and economic conditions; assisting minority communities to establish and strengthen constructive self-help and self-determination projects and programs; encouraging the involvement of minorities in the decision-making processes of their communities; and, promoting impartial law enforcement locally and encouraging compliance with federal law at all levels.

Occupation Information: Unlike most federal agencies concerned with civil and human rights, the CRS does not enforce laws, regulate practices, or grant funds for programs. It relies upon its professional staff, working out of six regional and thirty-two field offices, to persuade and encourage local citizens and institutions to take the initiative in solving their own problems. These field representatives, called Community Relations Specialists, are responsible for stimulating community relations in connection with civil rights activities. They assist communities in resolving disputes and other difficulties based upon racial discrimination. They meet with state and local officials; community leaders; national, regional, and local

114

civil rights groups to arrive at amicable solutions to problems of education, administration of justice, economic development, crises, and housing and planning. Community Relations Specialists in the Community Relations Service are in contact with the "real world" problems faced by members of minority groups in everyday life. They have the opportunity to deal directly with the problems and to contribute beneficially to resolving those problems. Community Relations Specialists begin at grade level GS-9 and below, depending on their experience and/or education.

Further Information—Write to: Administrative Office
Community Relations Service
U.S. Department of Justice
Washington, D.C. 20530

Relevant Bibliography Titles: 1, 8, 9, 14, 24, 25, 82, 94, 95, 98.

Department of Labor (DOL)
Manpower Administration

Nature and Purpose: The Manpower Administration consolidates all organizations and activities of the Department of Labor that direct, coordinate, or support manpower programs and operations so that improved and effective actions are directed toward achieving compatible objectives. The manpower programs of the Department of Labor cover a vast number of areas, from the funding of programs for retraining the hard-core unemployed, to helping returning veterans get needed job training, to maintaining a vast federal-state employment network and unemployment insurance program.

The agency's basic objective is to help the people of the United States realize their full employment potential. Therefore, the manpower operations include assisting individuals to adjust their skills to meet the constant changes in our economic needs. This includes retraining of people such as agricultural employees, older persons, the handicapped, and others displaced by technological changes. The Manpower Administration is also involved in a vast human resources development program—working with the unemployable to help them become useful citizens, working with youth to assist them in finding their place in the employment picture. In this area the Manpower Administration has become involved in recent years with such projects as the Neighborhood

115

Youth Corps, Concentrated Employment Programs, Youth Opportunity Centers, and many others.

Occupation Information: Two important positions in the manpower program area throughout the country are those of the Employment Service Adviser and the Manpower Development Specialist. Employment Service Advisers help in maintaining a federal-state system of public employment offices. In general, they assist in developing policies, standards, programs, and procedures in aiding employment security agencies. Some Advisers may deal with specific operating functions such as those involved in selecting and placing individual applicants with individual employers, or in finding employment for workers in geographic areas other than those in which they are currently employed. The agency's Manpower Development Specialists are concerned with programs pertaining to manpower resources, requirements, development, and utilization. They may plan, direct, or conduct activities, or act in an advisory capacity in regard to these programs. They may conduct activities related to industrial personnel management practices; industrial training and manpower utilization; occupational fields and industrial processes; job market conditions and trends and causes of unemployment; and qualification analyses and job requirements. For GS-5 and GS-7 positions, both Advisers and Specialists must have appropriate experience or a college degree in a related area. Staff members are assigned to either Washington, D.C., or regional offices.

Further Information—Write to: Manpower Administration
U.S. Department of Labor
Washington, D.C. 20120

Relevant Bibliography Titles: 9, 13, 43, 62, 71, 74, 76, 77, 95.

Department of Labor (DOL)
Occupational Safety and Health Administration(OSHA)

Nature and Purpose: The Occupational Safety and Health Administration, established in 1971, has broad responsibility for insuring that as far as possible every employee in the United States has safe and healthful working conditions. This requires setting workplace safety and health standards to protect 60 million workers in 5 million establishments, enforcing them, encouraging the states to adopt equally effective programs, conducting safety and health education and training, and conducting research into hazards, motivational factors, educational needs, and the like in conjunction with the National Institute for Occupational Safety and Health (an arm of the Department of Health, Education, and Welfare).

Occupation Information: In the area of enforcement, there are career opportunities in OSHA for Safety Officers and Industrial Hygienists. Safety Officers do research; develop and write procedures, directives, and instructions relating to the compliance manual; evaluate studies and resolve technical, administrative, and procedural problems involving standards and regulations; and research, review, and develop training course material for staff affecting compliance operations. Industrial Hygienists serve as resource persons and participate in the development of policies and procedures relating to the Target Health Hazards Program; they undertake special studies on Industrial Hygiene problems and evaluate the Industrial Hygiene program in all its aspects; they also maintain liaison with other federal and state agencies involved in occupational safety and health matters. Both of these positions are based in the agency's forty-nine Area Offices, but most time is spent away from the office inspecting establishments in the Area Office geographic area of responsibility. Entry levels are grades GS-9 and above, with greater education and experience requirements for the higher grades.

Further Information—Write to: Occupational Safety and Health Administration
U.S. Department of Labor
14th Street and Constitution Avenue, N.W.
Washington, D.C. 20210

Relevant Bibliography Titles: 9, 13, 43, 71, 77, 95.

Department of State (STATE)
Agency for International Development (A.I.D.)

Nature and Purpose: The Agency for International Development (A.I.D.) was created by Congress in 1961 to unify and administer existing foreign assistance programs. It is a semiautonomous branch of the State

Department with separate annual congressional legislation and funding.

By mutual agreement with approximately forty participating governments, A.I.D. provides a wide variety of assistance in development fields such as agriculture, education, industry, transportation, public administration, health, population, nutrition, and encourages participation of private business and private voluntary organizations. The focus is on the major needs and prerequisites for national development in low-income countries. The well-being of nations, an improvement in the quality of life for the average man through overall national and social and economic growth, is the goal. Today A.I.D. is at work in the developing countries of Asia, Africa, and Latin America.

Occupation Information:

A.I.D.'s overseas assistance programs require a wide range of professional and technical specialists. Agricultural economists work with the agriculture divisions of A.I.D. Missions and the Agriculture Ministries of host countries. They are involved in the development of systems to evaluate and improve production and distribution of agricultural products. A.I.D. education advisers assist in planning and budgeting education systems; designing school administration programs and procedures; developing curricula for all grade levels; preparing building specifications; training teachers and organizing programs to update methodology and improve teacher qualifications; training specialists in the production of textbooks and instructional materials. Engineers overseas assist in the preparation of feasibility studies, in project implementation, and in the supervising and monitoring of projects requiring expertise across the broad spectrum of engineering specialties. Medical Technologists help establish, equip, staff, and administer clinical diagnostic and public health laboratories. A.I.D. Public Health Nurses support health officials in the development of public health nursing programs country-wide. They help improve the quality of public health nursing practices, including administration, supervision, personnel utilization, and staff relationships. Public Health Physicians overseas plan, report, and evaluate health program activities within their assigned regions. They advise on health aspects of local programs, and coordinate public health activities with those of other divisions. Requirements for these positions are substantially the same as for similar positions in the public or private sector. Starting salaries are competitive, based on education and experience, and are supplemented by standard Foreign Service Allowances. Initial appointments overseas are usually for a tour of up to thirty months, including orientation, travel and overseas duty of twenty-four months.

Federal Agencies

Further Information—Write to: Professional Talent Search (ITB)
Office of Personnel & Manpower
Agency for International Development
Washington, D.C. 20523

Relevant Bibliography Titles: 2, 3, 6, 7, 11, 12, 42, 52, 53, 54, 60, 61, 63, 69, 70, 72, 73, 80, 83, 96, 102, 103.

Department of Transportation (DOT)
National Highway Traffic Safety Administration (NHTSA)

Nature and Purpose: The National Highway Traffic Safety Administration was established to carry out a congressional mandate to reduce the mounting number of deaths and injuries resulting from traffic accidents on the nation's highways. In accordance with these national goals the National Highway Traffic Safety Administration provides leadership to and coordination of programs to improve the safety of motor vehicles and components, pedestrian safety through education, and the problems of driver behavior that relate to safety.

It is part of NHTSA's mission to develop experimental safety vehicles whose safety features will be used as a basis for future motor vehicle safety standards. In addition, the agency is conducting an intensive information and education program to help identify and control the problem drinker.

NHTSA also develops safety standards and regulations for motor vehicles. In researching and developing these standards, the National Highway Traffic Safety Administration coordinates its activities with many agencies and industries and often relies on their resources. Among these are automobile manufacturers, research and development organizations, universities, and independent laboratories.

Occupation Information: NHTSA's personnel needs and requirements cover a broad spectrum of professional, technical, and vocational pursuits. They utilize the sciences of psychology, biology, mathematics, economics, medicine, law, optics, metallurgy, and almost every kind of engineering skill. Applicants should have an innovative approach and analytical minds. Long years of experience are not necessary, nor is it necessary to stay within one's own discipline. For in-

119

stance, engineers, mathematicians, physicists, and chemists may start as generalists in the intern program and seek another field of interest, such as research, testing, analysis, and so forth. Specialists in education, social science, health, and psychology work in research, human behavior, and many other areas. Headquarters is in Washington, D.C., and ten regional offices are manned by a technical staff which works directly with state and community officials.

Further Information—Write to:
Director of Personnel
National Highway Traffic Safety Administration
U.S. Department of Transportation
400 7th Street, S.W.
Washington, D.C. 20591

Relevant Bibliography Titles: 55, 71, 77, 95.

ACTION
Foster Grandparent Program (FGP)

Nature and Purpose:
The Foster Grandparent Program is a volunteer program providing opportunities for older persons to render supportive person-to-person services in health, education, welfare, and related settings to children having special needs. Currently, there are sixty-seven local projects in forty states and Puerto Rico with approximately 4,400 foster grandparents rendering person-to-person attention and service to 8,800 children daily. Over 200 different child care settings throughout the country are utilizing the services of foster grandparents.

Since 1965 the Foster Grandparent Program has offered to the older person an opportunity to serve and to live with increased self-esteem, independence, and sociability that is vital to the enjoyment of the later years. It has not only provided low-income older persons with a vastly improved standard of living but has demonstrated to society that older persons have the talent, skill, experience, and desire to serve their communities by meeting some of the unmet human needs in society.

Occupation Information:
Foster grandparents serve in health, education, and welfare settings, primarily in institutions. Grandparents usually serve two children, each for two hours a day, five days a week. They talk,

120

listen, read and sing to the children . . . cuddle an infant. Games, puzzles, and creative activities are encouraged. They give support and assistance to "their children" in learning and therapy situations. The foster grandparent creates an atmosphere in which a child is helped to grow emotionally, socially, and physically. In essence, a foster grandparent acts as a parent substitute for a child deprived of the benefits of a normal relationship with parents or older persons. To be a foster grandparent, a person must be aged sixty or over, with low income, physically able to serve, and willing to accept supervision. More important, perhaps, foster grandparents must care about children and want to help them. They receive a stipend of $1.60 per hour for their service. In addition, the foster grandparents are reimbursed for transportation costs and, where possible, are provided with a nutritious meal daily. They are covered by accident insurance and each foster grandparent receives an annual physical examination.

Further Information—Write to: Foster Grandparent Program
ACTION
806 Connecticut Avenue, N.W.
Washington, D.C. 20525

Relevant Bibliography Titles: 13, 20, 30, 50, 55, 77, 95.

ACTION
Peace Corps

Nature and Purpose: As legislated by the United States Congress in 1961 the Peace Corps was established to: help developing nations meet their needs for trained manpower; help promote better understanding of the American people on the part of people served; and promote a better understanding of other people on the part of the American people.

From the beginning, the Peace Corps has had one motivating idea. That people helping other people to help themselves is the most worthwhile way to promote peaceful development. To realize this mission, the Peace Corps arranges for the placement abroad of volunteer men and women of the United States in newly developed nations of the world to help fill their critical needs for skilled manpower. The Peace Corps serves only in those nations that request volunteers. Programs are developed by Peace

Corps staff and local people working with ministries and agencies within the host country. Volunteers also make inputs into new programs. The programs generally deal with the basic inhibitors of development—inadequate education, disease, malnutrition. Volunteers find themselves dealing with development in a most human way: training teachers and technicians; working in health and preventive medicine at the village level; trying to improve agriculture and food production by training farmers; improving small and medium-sized manufacturing in regions distant from capital cities.

Programs stress the achievement of specific goals—tuberculosis eradication in a particular area, for example, or the reorganization of a planning department in a small town. Most programs have a reasonable date for completion; the ideal is to finish a specific job and transfer the skill, leaving the task of continuing development in the hands of the local people.

There are now more than 8,500 Volunteers serving in fifty-six countries in some 540 separate projects.

Occupation Information: There are only two legal requirements for becoming a Peace Corps Volunteer: applicants must be at least eighteen years old (there is no upper age limit) and a United States citizen. A college degree is not required, but the Peace Corps looks for a skill or a particular level of education in each applicant to fit the requirements of available overseas positions. The kinds of Volunteers chosen are determined by the requests that originate in each of the host countries. Prior knowledge of a foreign language is not necessary. The Peace Corps gives its Volunteers twelve to fourteen weeks of training. Most tours, after training, are for twenty-four months. In country Volunteers live as their host-country people do and on an allotted living allowance. Allowances differ from country to country, and even within countries, because of cost-of-living differences. Worldwide, allowances vary from $69 per month in India to $160 per month in Togo. The average is $108. A readjustment fund of $75 per month is set aside for Volunteers in the United States and is payable at the completion of service.

Further Information—Write to: Peace Corps
Washington, D.C. 20525

OR

ACTION
Washington, D.C. 20525

Relevant Bibliography Titles: 2, 3, 6, 7, 31, 42, 44, 53, 54, 59, 60, 61, 63, 69, 70, 73, 80, 83, 93, 102, 103, 104.

ACTION
Smithsonian Institution-Peace Corps Environmental Program

Nature and Purpose: Environmental problems in the developing world are major, often crucial, obstacles to basic development and even to survival. The Smithsonian Institution has a combined program with the Peace Corps to place graduate students (and postdoctorals), skilled in the biological and environmental sciences, in appropriate assignments in the developing countries. The Volunteers in this program work under the direction of host-government agencies or are attached to scientific, conservation, or other organizations assisting or cooperating with the host country. The areas of scientific research include ecology, field biology, systematics, animal behavior, anthropology, preservation of endangered species, pollution control, conservation, and related environmental concerns.

Occupation Information: To be eligible, applicants should normally have completed candidate status for a master's degree or doctor's degree or hold such a degree. The assignments provide the opportunity for selected Volunteers to carry out field research that could be used to complete requirements for advanced degrees. The Smithsonian Institution participates in the selection and placement of the Volunteers and in some instances arranges specific technical support for the assignment. Assignments range over a very broad spectrum of scientific and technical fields—forestry, fisheries, wildlife management, ecological research, watershed management, environmental monitoring, air and water pollution research, water resource development, conservation education, and environmental health. Peace Corps programs presently operate in sixty countries. In addition, some Volunteers in environmental programs are attached to international organizations and serve in countries where there are no on-going Peace Corps programs. Tours are for twenty-four to twenty-seven months (including language training). In the case of environmental assignments, Volunteers are expected to possess their basic technical skills before being invited to training. Living allowances, covering

123

modest in-country living costs, vary according to the country of assignment. In addition, $75 per month is held in the United States for each Volunteer and is available at the conclusion of service.

Further Information: The standard Peace Corps application should be used, but for all environmental assignments, it should be mailed to:

Office of Ecology
Smithsonian Institution
Washington, D.C. 20560

To obtain a Peace Corps application, write to:

Director, Environmental Programs
Peace Corps
Washington, D.C. 20525

Relevant Bibliography Titles: 3, 18, 28, 31, 53, 59, 60, 73, 83, 102, 103.

ACTION
VISTA (Volunteers in Service to America)

Nature and Purpose: Vista (Volunteers in Service to America) is a national corps of Volunteers, men and women who work to alleviate poverty within the United States, including Hawaii and Alaska, and in Puerto Rico and the Virgin Islands. Vista was authorized by Congress in 1964. During any one year some 4,600 Volunteers are assigned for service to locally sponsored projects in urban ghettos, small towns, rural poverty areas, in the migrant streams, and on Indian Reservations.

A variety of public and private nonprofit organizations sponsor vista Volunteers. These include social welfare agencies; grass-roots neighborhood and community poverty organizations; city, county, and state agencies and other groups whose purposes are to assist people who are poor.

Occupation Information: Vista looks for Volunteers with the skills needed to assist the poor in solving the priority problems they have identified in their communities, whether in the area of health, economic development, education and manpower, housing, community planning, or social services. While there are no special educational or experience requirements, VISTA looks for Volunteers who have a particular understanding—the ability to communicate and help others to help themselves. Volunteers come from all age groups; however, few applicants under twenty years of age qualify for service. Great demands are placed on VISTA Volunteers, and they must have the maturity and experience to handle the difficult tasks of working in a poverty situation. After completing a four-to-six week training course, Volunteers are assigned to a project where they serve one full year. VISTA matches a Volunteer's skills, experience, and geographical preferences with the needs and demands of the sponsoring organizations. Volunteers receive a small stipend, just sufficient to support the Volunteer at a poverty level. In addition, $75 is set aside each month, and is paid to the Volunteer in a lump sum at the end of service.

Further Information—Write to:
VISTA
A part of ACTION
Office of Citizens Placement.
Washington, D.C. 20525

Relevant Bibliography Titles:
13, 31, 51, 59, 62, 77, 90, 94, 104, 105, 111.

Environmental Protection Agency (EPA)

Nature and Purpose:
The Environmental Protection Agency (EPA) was established December 2, 1970, and pulled together into one agency a variety of pollution control research, monitoring, and standards-setting activities that were previously scattered through several departments and agencies.

EPA is, first and foremost, a regulatory agency, with responsibilities for establishing and enforcing environmental standards, within the limits of its various statutory authorities. The standards set by EPA have the force of law. They define the kinds of levels of pollutants which must be prevented from entering our air and water, and establish timetables for achieving the prescribed quality. They set limits on radiation emissions and pesticide residues. Enforcement of environmental standards is, under certain laws, shared with the states, the federal government acting only when the state fails to do so; in other instances, the federal government has primary enforcement authority.

Effective action, particularly in standards-setting and enforce-

125

ment, requires that EPA have sound data on what is being introduced into the environment, its impact on ecological stability, on human health, and on other factors important to human life. By close coordination of its various research programs, EPA strives to develop a synthesis of knowledge from the biological, physical, and social sciences which can be interpreted in terms of total human and environmental needs.

In addition to performing research in its own laboratories, in various locations throughout the country, EPA, through grants and contracts, supports the studies of scientists in universities and other research institutions. The Agency also consolidates and evaluates information as it is developed throughout the scientific community to develop the best possible scientific base for environmental action. EPA serves also as a catalyst for environmental protection efforts at all levels of government by providing technical and financial assistance to state, regional, and local jurisdictions.

EPA publishes and gives wide distribution to its technical and scientific findings in all program areas, to advance the total body of scientific knowledge and hasten the application of new, proven pollution-control techniques. EPA also serves as a source of information to the public. By widely disseminating scientific data bearing on environmental problems, it tries to bring to concerned Americans the facts on which they, individually and in the community, can make sound, rational choices in environmental issues.

Occupation Information: To carry out the research aspects of the many environmental programs administered by EPA, a wide range of professions and skills are employed. Career opportunities are available in Air, Water, Radiation, Pesticide, Solid Waste Management, and Noise Abatement Programs for: physicists, chemists, biologists, engineers, urban planners, virologists, public health program specialists, entomologists, and many others. There are also career opportunities in the EPA enforcement and general counsel program for: attorneys who prepare legal briefs for enforcement actions against polluters; enforcement analysts who utilize their analytical ability in discerning violations and acting upon them; and engineers and chemists who are needed to analyze the technical aspects of key enforcement cases and assist the analyst in types of strategy to be used in the enforcement of imposed standards. Requirements for professional and administrative positions are at least four years of college and a bachelor's degree. On-the-job training is provided and in some cases supplemented by selected courses given within the Agency, and at other govern-

126

ment agencies. Salaries are competitive. EPA's headquarters are in Washington, D.C.; Regional Offices are located in ten major cities and are staffed by specialists in each program area. Most of EPA's research is carried out through three National Environmental Research Centers located at Cincinnati, Ohio; Research Triangle Park, North Carolina; and Corvallis, Oregon. The Centers direct and coordinate the work of satellite laboratories in various parts of the country.

Further Information—Write to: Environmental Protection Agency
Waterside Mall Building
4th and M Streets, S.W.
Washington, D.C. 20460

Relevant Bibliography Titles: 9, 13, 18, 23, 28, 71, 76, 77.

Federal Trade Commission (FTC)

Nature and Purpose: The basic objective of the Federal Trade Commission (FTC) is the maintenance of free competitive enterprise as the keystone of the American economic system. The Congress created the Commission in 1914 as an independent agency with broad powers to proceed in the public interest against unfair, deceptive, discriminatory, or monopolistic practices in interstate commerce.

The Commission is charged with responsibility for enforcing statutes designed to: promote free and fair competition through prevention of price-fixing agreements, boycotts, combinations in restraint of trade, and unfair or deceptive trade practices; safeguard the consuming public by outlawing false or misleading advertising and other fraudulent selling schemes; prevent discriminations in price, exclusive-dealing and tying arrangements, corporate mergers, and interlocking directorates when the effect of such practices or arrangements may be a substantial lessening of competition or a tendency toward monopoly; eliminate the payment or receipt of illegal brokerage, and eliminate discrimination among competing customers in the furnishing of, or payment for, advertising or promotional services or facilities; and to insure the truthful labeling of textiles and fur products, and prevent the marketing of dangerously flammable wearing apparel.

Occupation Information: As a law enforcement agency, the Federal Trade Commission employs attorneys in many phases of its operations. The work assignments of the legal staff reflect both the ultimate mission of the agency and its internal organization. Attorneys assigned to the Bureau of Consumer Protection exercise general surveillance over the legal aspects of the Commission's consumer protection activities. Those in the Bureau of Competition have responsibility for maintaining the integrity of the competitive economic system by enforcing those laws which are directed against monopoly and other trade restraining practices. The largest segment of the legal staff consists of attorneys assigned to field offices in eleven major cities where most of the legal case work of the Commission originates. The field office attorney is responsible for obtaining the evidence as to whether a law violation has occurred, evaluating this evidence, and making the initial recommendation as to action to be taken by the Commission. In addition, since many of the practices and problems which confront the Commission are economic, it is the function of economists in the Commission to gather and analyze the facts related to these problems and/or practices and then provide the Commission and sometimes the Congress with information and advice as to the proper action or policy to pursue. In the Division of Economic Evidence economists generally work closely with the Commission's attorneys in the investigation and trial of cases involving economic problems. Economists in the Division of Industry Analysis work on studies and reports which are concerned generally with the structure of a particular industry, a group of related industries, or with particular aspects of business conduct or performance. The Commission also has career opportunities for Consumer Protection Specialists, stationed in the field offices, who work to stop practices which deceive consumers. Specialists and economists must have a college degree or equivalent experience; entrance grades range from GS-5 to GS-11. Recent law school graduates, admitted to the bar of any state or the District of Columbia, are appointed as attorney grade GS-11. Experienced attorneys are appointed at higher grades.

Further Information—Write to: Director of Personnel
Federal Trade Commission
6th and Pennsylvania Ave., N.W.
Washington, D.C. 20580

Relevant Bibliography Titles: 13, 14, 23, 71, 76, 89.

Small Business Administration (SBA)

Nature and Purpose:

The Small Business Administration (SBA) is a permanent, independent government Agency created by Congress in 1953 to help small businesses grow and prosper. Congress directed SBA to insure free competition and to strengthen the overall economy of the nation. Through its network of field offices in the principal cities of every state as well as Guam and Puerto Rico, SBA offers small businesses financial assistance including lease guarantees, management assistance, aid in obtaining government contracts, counseling services, and publications covering successful practices in every small business field. In addition, SBA helps victims of disasters, and in a substantial way, broadens opportunities for individual imagination, initiative, and enterprise.

Occupation Information:

Career opportunities in SBA field offices are available in the functional area of financial assistance. Personnel in this area perform duties similar to those of loan officers in the banking industry. The types of loans made by the Agency include business, disaster, displaced business, economic opportunity, and development company loans. In the area of procurement and management assistance, specialists see that small business receives a fair share of government prime contracts and subcontracts and supply management counseling and training to small firms. While prior experience in the specialized areas is desirable, the Small Business Administration hires college graduates, with degrees in related areas, who can acquire the necessary skills on the job. These trainee positions are filled at the GS-5 and GS-7 levels.

Further Information—Write to:

Office of Personnel
Small Business Administration
1441 L Street, N.W.
Washington, D.C. 20416

Relevant Bibliography Titles:

9, 13, 76, 81.

U. S. Commission on Civil Rights (CCR)

Nature and Purpose:

The Commission on Civil Rights was established on September 9, 1957. It is a temporary, independent, bipartisan agency. The Commission on Civil Rights investigates complaints alleging that citizens are being deprived of their right to vote by reason of their race, color, religion, or national origin, or by reason of fraudulent practices; studies and collects information concerning legal developments constituting a denial of equal protection of the laws under the Constitution; appraises federal laws and policies with respect to equal protection of the laws; serves as a national clearinghouse for information in respect to denials of equal protection of the laws; and submits reports, findings, and recommendations to the President and the Congress.

Occupation Information:

To help carry out an important area of the Commission's responsibilities, a staff of Community Relations Specialists work with and advise local officials on programs relating to voting, public accommodations, public facilities, education, housing, and equal employment. They also work with State Advisory Committees in developing and analyzing information on problems in the Southern area. Another relevant position in the Agency is that of the Civil Rights Program Analyst. Personnel in this position assist in studies of the implementation by federal agencies of the civil rights policies in regard to denial of equal opportunities in education, employment, or housing; analyze statistical data; and prepare narrative conclusions. These positions require at least a bachelor's degree or the equivalent experience in the area of civil rights. On-the-job training is given at the GS-5 level. Personnel are stationed at headquarters in Washington, D.C., or in six field offices.

Further Information—Write to:

U.S. Commission on Civil Rights
1121 Vermont Avenue, N.W.
Washington, D.C. 20425

Relevant Bibliography Titles:

1, 8, 9, 13, 14, 24, 25, 71, 76, 94, 95, 98.

PART III

State Agencies

Alabama / Department of Conservation and Natural Resources

Nature and Purpose: The State Department of Conservation and Natural Resources is the service agency that watches over Alabama's natural resources. The wide-ranging responsibilities of the Department are divided among several Divisions. The Forestry Division administers 18,000,000 acres of forested lands. The State Lands Division gives supervision of both the lands within Alabama's parks and certain school lands defined in the Dominic-Young Act of 1939. Revenue from the lands is given to schools, hospitals, and conservation services. This Division also manages over 500,000 acres of subaqueous lands in river bottoms and the Gulf of Mexico. It is the responsibility of the Division of Water Safety to register and identify most of the 100,000 boats plying Alabama's waters. The Division also protects water-going persons and property with consistent law enforcement and a far-flung safety education program. A Bureau of Parks and Recreation manages Alabama's fourteen state parks which are located in every section of the state and include over 36,000 acres. The Game and Fish Division administers twenty-seven refuges and game management areas, as well as twenty county fishing lakes. The Division of Seafoods supervises laws and regulations pertaining to seafoods.

Occupation Information: A cross section of personnel important to the various functions of the Department includes the following: Biologists who are employed in a variety of field and laboratory projects connected with fish and game conservation; Conservation Enforcement Officers who are responsible for the enforcement of conservation laws pertaining to fish and game, seafood, or water safety; Park

133

Rangers who participate in a wide variety of tasks necessary to the proper maintenance and protection of land and water areas, buildings, and other physical improvements at parks and historical sites; Park Managers who plan and direct the operations of state parks with recreation facilities; Game Refuge Managers who are responsible for the operation of game areas established for the protection and propagation of wildlife; and Lands Inspectors who manage the state-owned lands used for conservation and other purposes. While previous experience is required for all these positions, graduation from high school is the minimum educational requirement for all except Biologists and Park Managers who must have a college degree.

Further Information—Write to: Department of Conservation and Natural Resources
State Administrative Building
64 North Union Street
Montgomery, Alabama 36104

Relevant Bibliography Titles: 9, 13, 18, 23, 28, 95.

Alabama / Department of Pensions and Security

Nature and Purpose: The Department of Pensions and Security has broad responsibilities for administering all forms of public assistance; for services to adults and to children and their families; and for working with other agencies in behalf of people. The agency has both specific and implied legal responsibilities. A county department is located in each of Alabama's 67 counties, usually in the county seat. Direct services are provided there, including approval for aid. In the state Department, work is carried forward through nine divisions or bureaus, as follows: Administrative Services; Informational Service; Accounts; Research and Statistics; Public Assistance; Field Service; Child Welfare; Commodity Distribution; and Staff Development.

The largest operation of the Department, both in terms of money spent and of people benefiting, is the program of financial aid or public assistance. This provides money payments to needy people who meet the requirements for one of the "categories" of aid and social services to adults. The agency also has a responsibility to help any child who needs it to gain a "fair opportunity in life," including those in the families receiving Aid to Dependent

Children. In addition, the Department is legally responsible for administering emergency welfare services for any Alabamian affected by any major emergency.

Occupation Information: The Alabama Department of Pensions and Security employs persons to fill social work positions in all 67 counties and the State department. From beginning positions as Case Worker I and Child Welfare Worker I, they range upward in qualifications and responsibilities to those of Administrative Assistant and Bureau Director on the state staff and Director in the counties. Case Workers I initiate services for persons seeking financial aid or social services or both. In entry level positions, Child Welfare Workers counsel parents about their children and deal with a variety of children's problems. The annual salary for the beginning social work position starts at $6,877 to the top social work job having a salary of $18,018. The requirements for social work positions vary from the beginning level baccalaureate degree requirements to a master's degree in social work. For jobs in between these levels, there are positions which require a combination of graduate training and some experience in a social work capacity. Progressively more education and experience, some of the latter in special areas, are necessary for supervisory and administrative positions.

Further Information—Write to: Personnel Unit
State Department of Pensions and Security
Montgomery, Alabama 36104

Relevant Bibliography Titles: 9, 13, 26, 27, 29, 32, 41, 55, 62, 75.

Alaska / Department of Health and Social Services

Nature and Purpose: The Department of Health and Social Services is a single all-inclusive administrative entity dedicated to the proposition of protecting and enhancing the health and well-being of all Alaskans. The Department's goal is the complete unification and integration of programs to provide professional preventive medical, psychiatric, nursing, social, custodial, environmental, and rehabilitative services to all Alaskans.

Organizationally, the Department is divided into six major functional elements. They are (1) General Administration,

(2) Public Health, (3) Public Welfare, (4) Environmental Health, (5) Corrections, and (6) Mental Health. General Administration exists to support, promote, and give service to the five program elements which act in harmony to provide a broad spectrum of social services. The Division of Public Health is responsible for promoting positive good health for every Alaskan. Programs are directed at the prevention of illness, early detection of disease, and constant surveillance for incipient epidemics. The Division of Public Welfare has responsibility for the administration of all public welfare activities in the state. This includes: federal grant-in-aid programs; the General Relief program; the General Relief Medical Care program; and social services to children committed to the Department. The Division of Environmental Health is responsible for promoting health and welfare through control of the various aspects of the environment with which man comes in contact. The Division of Corrections has the responsibility for the operation of state programs designed for the care and treatment of adult offenders and delinquents plus programs for prevention and control of crime and delinquency. The Division of Mental Health is responsible for the development and administration of a complete and comprehensive program for the prevention of mental illness and the care and treatment of persons who are mentally ill, including inpatient and outpatient care and treatment of such persons.

Occupation Information: A wide variety of professional, administrative, and technical personnel carry out the various missions of the Department of Health and Social Services. The Division of Public Health requires the services of personnel trained in the professions of medicine, public health nursing, microbiology, health education, social work, and public health administration. The staff engages in direct services and demonstrations of personal and community health management. Services of the Division of Public Welfare are provided through a staff of social workers who deal with many complex and diversified social problems such as adoption, foster home care, child welfare, and medical and family assistance. The Environmental Health program is carried out through regional offices, each staffed with professional environmental engineers and sanitarians. The Division of Corrections furnishes probation services to the entire state through a staff of probation officers who are assigned investigative, guidance, and supervisory responsibilities. Further counseling, group guidance, and psychological services are provided to youthful and adult offenders by psychological counselors and youth counselors. The Department's mental health program affords career opportunities to medical and nursing personnel, psychiatric and medical social workers, psychologists, and many others. Education and experience requirements for positions mentioned above vary depending on the duties performed and the level of administrative responsibility assumed. Salaries are competitive, with a 7 percent cost-of-living difference added in the Northwestern and Central Districts (Fairbanks and Nome). Places of assignments are varied and are scattered across the state.

Further Information—Write to: Department of Health and Social Services
Personnel Office
Pouch H
Juneau, Alaska 99801

Relevant Bibliography Titles: 9, 13, 19, 22, 23, 28, 29, 30, 32, 33, 41, 57, 66, 75, 110.

Arkansas / Employment Security Division / Work Incentive Program (WIN)

Nature and Purpose: The WIN program, administered by the Employment Security Division, is designed to deliver manpower services to recipients of Aid to Families with Dependent Children (AFDC) who are able-bodied and not in school. The program offers job placement, training, or special work project opportunities to assist these persons to become self-sufficient. The Arkansas program began in June of 1968 and now includes thirty-one counties and 1,080 enrollee slots.

Occupation Information: Important members of each Employment Security Division WIN team includes a counselor, a job developer, a work training specialist, and an orientation instructor. As referrals are received from the various county units of the Social Services Division, individual employability development plans are developed by the team of specialists. The various services outlined in the plan are then delivered to the enrollee. Through the benefit of these services, the enrollee is enabled to move from public assistance into meaningful employment. Requirements for positions on the WIN team include a college degree and/or graduate work or experience in a related area. Beginning salaries range from $500 to $600 per month, depending on which position in the team

137

new employees are assigned to. WIN project offices are located in five cities throughout the state.

Further Information—Write to:

Arkansas Employment Security Division
P. O. Box 2981
Little Rock, Arkansas 72203

Relevant Bibliography Titles:

9, 13, 32, 41, 43, 58, 62, 71, 74, 75, 95.

California / Department of Conservation / California Ecology Corps

Nature and Purpose:

The California Ecology Corps, established on July 1, 1971, allows California's government to increase its efforts in protecting the state's environment. Secondly, the Corps permits the Department of Conservation to draw on selected young men who have volunteered to become a trained work force involved in numerous conservation projects.

The Corps: recruits and employs members to aid in the maintenance of the natural ecology and the preservation of the beauty and natural resources of California; utilizes its members in conservation and emergency projects to effect full utilization and protection of the natural resources for the greatest possible number of people; assists in the protection of natural resources, which includes, but is not limited to, forests, grasses, vegetation, soil, air, water, wildlife, recreational and scenic resources; and assists in fire prevention and fire protection.

Occupation Information:

Although the executive order which established the Corps is open-ended with regard to the type of volunteer acceptable for the program, the Department of Conservation has worked with the Selective Service System to recruit young men classified by their draft boards as "conscientious objectors" to armed military duty. Service in the Corps, however, is now also available to other volunteers. Under the direction of the Department of Conservation and the supervision of the Division of Forestry, Corpsmen engage in a wide array of conservation projects, in addition to basic firefighting responsibilities. Volunteers should be willing to commit themselves for six months or a year. Corpsmen receive a monthly allowance of approximately $100. In addition, the corpsmen receive room and board, certain personal care items, work clothing, and other supplies. Assignments are at one of four Ecology Centers in the state.

Further Information—Write to:

California Ecology Corps
Department of Conservation
1416 Ninth Street
Sacramento, California 95814

Relevant Bibliography Titles:

9, 14, 18, 23, 28, 31, 46, 47, 48, 59, 104.

California / Department of Corrections

Nature and Purpose:

The Department of Corrections administers the state's correctional system for adults convicted of felonies and committed by the courts to the Director of Corrections for terms prescribed by law. More than 23,000 inmates are kept under custody and treated in the state institutions operated by the Department of Corrections. The Department also participates in the operation of highway and forestry honor camps where more than 1,500 inmates work. In addition, the Department of Corrections operates the state's treatment-control program for civilly committed narcotics addicts.

While the primary responsibility of the Department is the safe and sure custody of offenders, it emphasizes a program of treatment designed to help each inmate to become prepared vocationally, academically, physically, psychologically, and spiritually to take his place in free society.

Occupation Information:

There are approximately 6,800 employees in the Department of Corrections, assigned to various professional, technical, or administrative areas. Positions within the area of educational programs include Arts and Crafts, Elementary, High School, Music, and Recreation and Physical Education Teachers. Through these teachers a wide range of academic and vocational courses are offered to nearly 12,000 inmates. Other key personnel in the rehabilitation program of the Department are: Correctional Counselors who assemble, organize, analyze, and record information necessary for classification and parole planning for prison inmates; they also interview and counsel inmates and assist with their adjustment and plans for rehabilitation in a correctional setting. Correctional Officers who supervise inmates on work

139

assignments, at recreation, and in the living units, and are responsible for their control and discipline. And Parole Agents who carry a case load involving office and field work in the supervision and guidance of adult parolees from state correctional institutions. Requirements for teacher, correctional counselor, and parole agent positions are graduation from college and related experience. Entry level positions require a minimum amount of previous experience. Correctional officers are required to have an education equivalent to completion of the twelfth grade and related experience. Salaries are competitive. Assignments are at thirteen major institutions or at fifty Parole and Community Services Offices located throughout the state.

Further Information—Write to: State of California
Department of Corrections
714 P Street, Office Building No. 8
Sacramento, California 95814

Relevant Bibliography Titles: 9, 19, 43, 56, 76, 77, 95.

California / Department of Housing and Community Development

Nature and Purpose: The Department of Housing and Community Development was established on September 17, 1965. It was created with two divisions, a Division of Research and Assistance, and a Division of Codes and Standards. The Department has the following program objectives: to promote and maintain adequate housing and decent living environments for California's citizens of all socio-economic levels; to protect the public from inadequate construction, manufacture, repair, or rehabilitation of buildings, particularly dwelling units, and from improper living environments through the establishment and enforcement of health and safety standards; and to serve as a catalyst in seeking solutions to California's housing and community development problems through technical assistance, advice, research, and dissemination of information to citizens, private industry, and governmental entitities. The first objective is a general one, common to both of the Department's two divisions, while the second is within the authority of the Division of Codes and Standards, and the third, the Division of Research and Assistance.

Occupation Information: To carry out the goals of the Division of Research and Assistance, a staff of Community Development Representatives are stationed in three field offices located in population centers in the state. Employees in this class perform a wide variety of technical assistance and research work in carrying out a program of assistance to all types of local governmental agencies and private organizations in the fields of housing development, housing finance, and community development. Incumbents serve as field representatives providing advice and assistance in the interpretation of the policies of the Department and laws and regulations concerning government housing and community development programs. They process requests for assistance; compile the necessary information and justifications for applying for financial assistance for housing and community improvement projects; collect and analyze data relative to the housing needs of the people in various income groups; and research and develop proposals for new or revised governmental programs or regulations which will improve housing conditions. Requirements for this position include graduation from college with a major in urban or regional planning, or a comparable field. In addition, varying amounts of experience are needed for all but the entry level position in this class. Salaries range from $692 a month for Community Development Representative I to $1,243 a month for Community Development Representative IV.

Further Information—Write to: State of California
Department of Housing and Community Development
Personnel Office
1121 O Street
Sacramento, California 95814

Relevant Bibliography Titles: 9, 13, 71, 82, 95.

California / Department of Rehabilitation

Nature and Purpose: The Department of Rehabilitation assists and encourages persons with physical and mental handicaps to prepare for and engage in gainful employment or useful service to the extent of their capabilities and subsequently to increase their full social and economic well-being.

Since the Department was formed, in 1963, services have been provided to disabled persons who are unemployed, underemployed, or whose employment is threatened by the progress of the disability and who show a reasonable promise that the assistance available will enable them to return to work. Basically the Department's programs offer vocational diagnosis and evaluation, guidance, counseling, training, and various other services, as needed, to bring disabled persons to the point of employment. The client's placement and follow-up in a permanent job are the final goals.

A variety of rehabilitation services to help young adults and older persons who are blind or nearly blind is also a part of the Department's basic program. Designed to help them to adjust to their visual disability and to help them become employed, these services include prevocational training; adjustment services to the adult blind in their homes and in the community by counselor-teachers and to high school youth by orientation and mobility specialists; and industrial rehabilitation services providing work adjustment, work experience, job training, and employment for the blind and otherwise handicapped persons. The Department's Business Enterprise Program for the Blind trains and establishes blind persons in business as operators of snack bars, cafeterias, and vending stands.

Occupation Information:

Vocational Rehabilitation Counselors are the center of California's vocational rehabilitation programs. The counselor carries the responsibility for evaluating the extent of vocational handicap and for developing residual abilities in the disabled. Most counselors work with a general caseload of some one hundred clients. There is an opportunity for specialization for those interested in such groups as the alcoholic, blind, deaf and hard of hearing, disabled public school students, mentally ill, mentally retarded, public assistance recipients, severely disabled, and public offenders (parolees). For Job Development Specialists, in addition, there are career opportunities in the major metropolitan areas. Vocational Rehabilitation Counselors in the Disability Determination Program are at the same classification level as those in the Vocational Rehabilitation Program. They function as part of the adjudication team which consists of a medical consultant and a counselor. This work involves evaluation of vocational and medical information to determine if the mental or physical disability of a claimant prevents his working in gainful employment. At present the Vocational Rehabilitation Program employs more than 400 counselors and the Disability Determination Program has a staff of nearly 150 counselors. A master's degree in rehabilitation counseling or a baccalaureate degree plus two years of vocational counseling experience are required for counselor positions. Trainee positions, in this class, require only a college degree. Salaries begin at $8,112 a year for trainees and at $10,440 for counselors. The Department's services are provided in field offices throughout the state and in vocational rehabilitation units in various state mental hospitals, state correctional institutions, school districts, alcoholism clinics, community mental health programs, and in the California School for the Deaf, and the California School for the Blind.

Further Information—Write to:

State of California
Department of Rehabilitation
714 P Street
Sacramento, California 95814

Relevant Bibliography Titles:

9, 13, 21, 30, 32, 33, 41, 55, 65, 67, 71, 77, 95.

Connecticut / Department of Children and Youth Services

Nature and Purpose:

The Department of Children and Youth Services, established in 1969, is responsible for creating, developing, operating, and administering a comprehensive and integrated statewide program for children and youth whose behavior does not conform to the law or to acceptable community standards. Presently, the Department operates two institutions for adjudicated delinquent children. However, a major thrust of the Department's program is work with children early, before minor problems turn into major ones, and in the community wherever possible. By working with children in their communities, it is hoped that with appropriate supervision and counseling, such youth can begin to adjust to their community and cope with the problems which arise there.

Occupation Information:

The Department of Children and Youth Services offers the college graduate a career with opportunities for total involvement in many of the social problem areas facing society today. Since the Department's emphasis is rehabilitative care, each employee becomes a vital part of the effort to effect change in those problems affecting youth today. A recently developed staff position, vital to the mission of the Department, is that of the Youth Services Officer. As a paraprofessional counselor who functions

143

within a comprehensive program of rehabilitative care, the Youth Services Officer helps bridge the communications gap between the child in his care and society. In residential living assignments such as in cottage life or a treatment center, the Youth Services Officer advises and counsels individual youth as well as groups. In cooperation with other professional staff members such as teachers, psychologists, vocational instructors, and social workers, the Youth Services Officer tailors the programs of rehabilitative care to suit a particular youth's needs. The primary function of the Youth Services Officer is to help a youngster develop a sense of self-awareness and confidence. He or she serves as a translator, defining while helping to solve the problems affecting today's youth. They also work closely with the Juvenile Court authorities, volunteer organizations, and other civic groups. Salaries for Youth Services Officers begin at $7,622 annually. A number of career opportunities make it possible for the Youth Services Officer to eventually earn up to $15,000 per year.

Further Information—Write to: Department of Children and Youth Services
Personnel Office
345 Main Street
Hartford, Connecticut 06115

Relevant Bibliography Titles: 9, 15, 30, 32, 55, 58, 67, 77.

Connecticut / Department of Community Affairs (DCA)

Nature and Purpose: The Department of Community Affairs (DCA) was created in 1967 to improve the conditions and quality of urban life. The Department exists to meet the needs of Connecticut's people by providing the services and facilities they require, and by attacking the causes of the state's problems. Its scope of powers and duties extends over some of the most controversial but vital issues in local government today—from changing a community's physical makeup to developing its human resources.

DCA operates on the principle that activities can be performed best at the lowest feasible level of government. In its attempt to improve the conditions of community life, it considers local autonomy and initiative to be of prime importance. The Department works with local governments which have neither the resources nor the tax bases equal to the task. DCA assists where local personnel, expertise, or money is lacking in the development of programs, the securing of funds (both state and federal), the operation of programs, and the evaluation of them. The Department has tried to confront problems through partnership in planning and action. This has included: the establishment of such local agencies as human resources development agencies, housing authorities, or community development action plan agencies that can effectively attack the problems; the mobilization of resources to make effective the role of a local agency in a community through the provision of information and guidance regarding available programs and strategies, assistance in the development of programs often through program studies or the preparation of simulation models, and through the increasing use of local competence and expertise; the maintenance of programs through state technical and financial assistance, supportive facts and information, and assistance in the obtaining of federal grants; and the evaluation of program results through analysis of their costs and benefits and other appropriate measures that will help DCA in the development of new programs in similar areas.

Occupation Information: The Department of Community Affairs' Bureau of Program Development and Community Services provides the continuing contacts with local governments and municipal officials. A staff of community development generalists is employed in five geographic districts and provides technical assistance to municipalities. In addition, these generalists are responsible for coordinating the development of grant-in-aid applications for state assistance. Included in the district staffs are sub-professional staff members possessing the unique talents required to communicate with the state's inner-city residents. These Neighborhood Resource Workers act as representatives of the agency in establishing basic communications with neighborhood individuals and groups for the purpose of identifying services needed, and the availability of agency assistance and resources to meet these needs. Education and experience requirements vary for the above positions. Progressively more education and/or experience are required as positions increase in responsibility and complexity of duties.

Further Information—Write to: Department of Community Affairs
Personnel Department
1179 Main Street
Hartford, Connecticut 06103

145

Relevant Bibliography Titles: 9, 13, 71, 82, 94, 104.

Delaware / Division of Drug Abuse

Nature and Purpose:

The Division of Drug Abuse, established in 1970, is charged with two major responsibilities—coordination of all drug abuse treatment for the drug abuser and prevention through drug education.

Occupation Information:

The Division's Drug Counseling Unit offers career opportunities for Addiction Counselors. These counselors are responsible for interviewing and counseling persons with drug or alcohol related problems, and for participating in and assisting in supervising the care of aggressively disturbed drug or alcoholic patients at state facilities or programs. Counselor I positions require graduation from high school and two years' work in a college or university, or two years of experience in social services or community affairs. Counselor II positions require graduation from a college or university and one year of experience in a drug or alcoholism related field. The beginning salary for Counselor I is $5,600 annually; Counselor II begins at $6,500.

Further Information—Write to:

State Office of Drug Abuse
3000 Newport Gap Pike
Wilmington, Delaware, 19808

Relevant Bibliography Titles: 9, 10, 13, 23, 32, 34, 66, 67, 71, 110.

Delaware / Division of Youth Affairs

Nature and Purpose:

The Division of Youth Affairs was formed in 1970. It was given the role of involving youth in all levels of public and private sectors. A youth-oriented staff has the responsibility of getting all segments of the youth community involved in programs and projects designed by the youth. In addition, the youth-oriented staff involves decision-making adults with the youth changes.

146

Occupation Information: The Division's activities are carried forward by two classes of advisers. Working directly with the youth and adults in the community are Youth Program Advisers who organize and involve youth in the functions of the government. They are supervised by Program Advisers who are also responsible for planning, coordinating, and conducting programs of volunteer youth activities. Youth Program Advisers are required to have two years of advanced education from a college or university, or, instead of schooling, two years of specialized training in a related area. Program Advisers must be college graduates with some experience in community development and social programming. Youth Program Adviser salaries range from $5,600 to $7,250 annually, while Program Adviser salaries range from $8,200 to $13,300 annually.

Further Information—Write to: Division of Youth Affairs
Room 302 Arden Building
11 North Street
Dover, Delaware 19901

Relevant Bibliography Titles: 9, 13, 15, 27, 32, 55, 58, 67, 77.

Indiana / Civil Rights Commission

Nature and Purpose: The Indiana Civil Rights Commission exists to eliminate discrimination because of race, religion, color, sex, national origin, or ancestry in education, employment, housing, and public accommodations.

Occupation Information: The Civil Rights Commission utilizes workers from Neighborhood Youth Corps and VISTA Volunteers. Its own staff varies from clerical to professional—primarily investigators, attorneys, and administrators. Requirements range from less than a high school education to a law degree. Some training is given all personnel on-the-job. At present all employees are stationed in Indianapolis and overnight travel throughout the state is required of professional staff members. Salaries range from $3,600 to $20,000 per year.

Further Information—Write to: State of Indiana
Civil Rights Commission
215 North Senate Avenue
Indianapolis, Indiana 46202

147

Relevant Bibliography Titles: 1, 8, 9, 10, 13, 14, 24, 25, 32, 71, 77, 95, 98.

Kansas / Department of Labor / Employment Security Division

Nature and Purpose: The Employment Security Division is responsible for employment service programs and unemployment insurance. Through its Employment Service Offices the following programs and services are made available: Job Placement; Job Bank; Aptitude Testing; Manpower Training; Services for the Handicapped, Veterans, and Older Workers; Farm and Rural Program; WIN; Counseling; and Apprenticeship Information. Unemployment benefits are provided under the Employment Security program from funds contributed entirely by employers. These benefits are designed to tide eligible workers over temporary periods of unemployment while they are trying to find jobs.

Occupation Information: There are three positions, normally entry level jobs, which embody the basic services provided by the Employment Security Division—Interviewer, Claims Examiner, and Counselor. Interviewers provide the first level of service to unemployed persons seeking aid in finding work. They must be knowledgeable of the Employment Service practices and procedures. The Interviewer needs to be aware of job opportunities and labor market conditions prevalent in the area. He should be able to spot vocational problems which need special attention. Above all the Interviewer should be an individual who understands people and can communicate well with them. The requirement for entry is a college degree in psychology, sociology, business, or a related field; some substitution is allowed for related work experience. The Claims Examiner deals with claims for unemployment insurance. In Kansas, as in most states, if a person worked under employment covered by the Employment Security Law and is out of work due to no fault of his own, he is eligible to receive unemployment benefits. The Claims Examiner aids individuals thus affected, and accepts their initial claims for unemployment insurance. He must have the ability to communicate well with people and have a basic understanding of the Unemployment Insurance Law. The requirements for entry to the Claims Examiner position is similar to that of the Interviewer. In the Job Opportunity Center setting, the Counselor deals mainly with people who have employ-

148

ment problems or with young people who are in the process of selecting a vocation. He must be cognizant of counseling and testing procedures, and have the ability to communicate with people, especially disadvantaged individuals who need special help in finding and keeping employment. The requirements for this position are a college degree, preferably with a major in psychology, and fifteen hours of graduate work in guidance or counseling.

Further Information—Write to:

State of Kansas
Labor Department
Employment Security Division
401 Topeka Avenue
Topeka, Kansas 66603

Relevant Bibliography Titles: 9, 13, 32, 95.

Kentucky / Commission on Human Rights

Nature and Purpose:

The Commission on Human Rights encourages fair treatment of all persons. Commission services include: research, study, and investigation of reports of discrimination; investigation of complaints; and seeking appropriate relief in circuit courts.

Occupation Information:

An important part of the agency's mission is carried out by a staff of Human Rights Representatives. Their duties reflect the various areas of responsibility found within the Commission on Human Rights. They conduct research on matters coming before the Commission; gather information on the continued existence of discrimination in Kentucky and on the extent and success of desegregation; analyze the statutes and regulations governing the operation of various state agencies as they relate to the "Governor's Code of Fair Practice" and assist in negotiations with heads of state departments and agencies to insure implementation of the Governor's Code; perform research and analysis on proposed legislation concerning human rights; assist in the investigation and conciliation of complaints received by the Commission and in complaints of discrimination in employment by contractors through conferences with their management and personnel directors; provide follow-up guidance and counsel to community groups about available facts and the most successful methods for

149

community activities to promote human rights; and occasionally speak to civic, community, and religious groups to disseminate information regarding desegregation. The minimum qualification for entry in this position is graduation from an accredited college or university with a bachelor's degree in the social sciences, or a closely related field. Salaries are competitive.

Further Information—Write to:

Commission on Human Rights
Capitol Annex
Frankfort, Kentucky 40601

Relevant Bibliography Titles:

1, 8, 9, 13, 14, 24, 25, 32, 71, 77, 95, 98.

Kentucky / Department of Child Welfare

Nature and Purpose:

The Department of Child Welfare, established in 1960, locates and plans for all children who are dependent, neglected, abandoned, delinquent, or in danger of becoming delinquent; cooperates with and assists the juvenile and circuit courts in matters relating to children; and performs other services necessary for the welfare of children, including the operation of treatment institutions for delinquent and emotionally disturbed children.

The Kentucky Department of Child Welfare currently provides the following services: Adoption; Foster Care; Services to Delinquent Children; Services to the Emotionally Disturbed; Homemaker Services; Services to Physically Abused Children; Protective Services; Group Homes; Day Care; Services to Unmarried Parents; Institutional Care; and Preventive Services.

Occupation Information:

The Department of Child Welfare offers career opportunities for those interested in working with children and young people. A bachelor's level social worker may work in the area of adoptions, juvenile delinquency, foster care, protective services, or family services. A social worker in an institution works with the rehabilitation of children both on an individual and group basis. Juvenile Counselors do probationary service and counseling for juvenile delinquents and their families, and plan and make recommendations for treatment. Any degree is acceptable for these positions. Social workers with a master's degree and social work experience perform more comprehensive case work, both field and institutional, or they may function as a specialist in the central office, or as an Assistant Superintendent of Institutions. Salaries are competitive.

Further Information—Write to: Department of Child Welfare
403 Wapping
Frankfort, Kentucky 40601

Relevant Bibliography Titles: 9, 13, 15, 27, 30, 32, 33, 41, 55, 58, 67, 77.

Kentucky / Department of Corrections

Nature and Purpose: The Kentucky Department of Corrections is charged with rehabilitation of adult felons committed to its care through counseling, education, and vocational training; and the security of those confined for the protection of society. In addition, responsibilities of the Department range from the supervision of a statewide probation and parole system to the operation of state correctional institutions. Providing administrative cohesion for all institutional programs is a Division of Institutions.

Occupation Information: Social service career opportunities, in the Department, exist in a wide range of programs. Expansion in recent years has included the improvement of the education program at each institution through employment of qualified and professional educators; improvement of medical and psychological services through a staff of psychologists, counselors, and doctors; initiation of social services programs administered by beginning and experienced social workers and the appointment of training officers for purposes of administering in-service programs. One of the department's programs is administered through the Division of Probation and Parole which offers field services and provides the basic case history on all subjects. Recent college graduates assigned as Probation and Parole Officers supervise parolees and probationers and encourage them to improve their conduct and social and economic conditions. Officers, with a degree supplemented by two years of responsible experience in the field, supervise, counsel, and direct persons paroled to regional jurisdiction. They also conduct interviews and criminal interrogations. The positions described above are located in the facilities under the Department's supervision or in nine district field offices with the Division of Probation and Parole.

151

Further Information—Write to: Kentucky Department of Corrections
State Office Building
Frankfort, Kentucky 40601

Relevant Bibliography Titles: 9, 19, 43, 56, 76, 77, 95.

Kentucky / Department of Economic Security

Nature and Purpose: The principal concern of the Department of Economic Security is to administer a coordinated social security program dedicated primarily to maintaining family unity and a reasonable measure of economic security for family units during periods of economic and social distress resulting from such circumstances as unemployment, disability, absence of the family wage earner, old age, ill health, death, and problems concerning children; and to the extent possible giving services designed to restore family units to a state of independence and self-sufficiency. From the standpoint of economic self-sufficiency, clients of the department are classified into three categories: unemployable, potentially employable, and employable. Programs are tailored to the needs of these three classifications.

The Employment Service Division of the Department is responsible for programs designed to give those who are unemployed, disadvantaged, and underemployed the employment assistance they need to prepare them to the point where they can compete successfully in today's job market.

The Unemployment Insurance Division provides unemployment benefits to persons who are unemployed through no fault of their own, have held a substantial attachment to the labor force, and are able to work and available to work. Unemployment insurance is a program for income maintenance during periods of involuntary unemployment due to lack of work; it provides partial compensation of wage loss as a matter of right.

The Public Assistance Program, administered by the Public Assistance Division, provides needy persons with income to supplement their own resources; to enable them to secure the necessities of life and medical and remedial care and services; to help them achieve the greatest economic and personal independence possible to them; and to enable them to remain in their own homes as family units.

Occupation Information: The Department of Economic Security offers a broad scope of career opportunities, appealing to various academic orientations and interests. Social worker positions, requiring a bachelor's degree without previous qualifying experience, include Field Workers, Service Workers, Food Stamp Workers, and WIN Workers. The main task of the field worker is to determine eligibility of the client, provide financial assistance, help the client to recognize and use his resources, and to obtain needed services from community resources. The service worker provides more intensive counseling services to troubled clients. His duties consist of professional counseling services to children and adults with economic, social, physical, and emotional problems. Food stamp workers determine client eligibility for the food stamp program and accept and review applications in the county public assistance offices. The WIN (Work Incentive Program) worker refers AFDC clients for enrollment in Work Incentive training programs and also counsels these same clients before, during, and after training. Positions requiring a college degree and one or more years of related experience include Social Worker II through VI positions. Beginning Social Workers, in this series, interview, evaluate, and provide appropriate professional social work services for clients with emotional, social, physical, or mental problems or disorders. Experienced Social Workers have greater administrative and technical responsibilities. Other positions, having the same educational and experience requirements, include: Food Stamp Field Representatives who supervise and coordinate field operations in a multi-county area for the food stamp program; and Community Relations and Licensing Representatives who interpret, apply, and enforce laws and approved policies of the department pertaining to licensing of homes for the aged. The Department of Economic Security also employs a great number of individuals who are skilled in various other academic disciplines. A variety of employment opportunities exist within the department for attorneys, Employment Interviewers, Employment Counselors, and many others. New employees of the Department receive basic orientation to its programs and continuing training is offered in such areas as casework relationships, communication, mental illness and retardation, and unmarried parenthood.

Further Information—Write to: Department of Economic Security
Director of Personnel & Training
New Capitol Annex
Frankfort, Kentucky 40601

153

Relevant Bibliography Titles: 9, 13, 26, 29, 32, 41, 55, 67, 75, 77, 95.

Maine / Environmental Improvement Commission

Nature and Purpose: The Maine Environmental Improvement Commission is the pollution control agency of the state. Its program consists of water pollution control, air pollution control, site development control, and oil conveyance control.

Occupation Information: Career opportunities are available in the Environmental Improvement Commission for persons trained in the field of engineering (sanitary, civil, chemical); in the field of chemistry; and in the field of biology. Varying degrees of education and experience are required for positions in these fields. Most assignments are based at Augusta, but a small number are in other cities of Maine. Salaries per annum in professional engineer positions are generally from $9,700 to $21,000; for engineering technicians from $7,000 to $13,500; for chemists from $7,300 to $13,500; and for biologists from $8,000 to $15,000.

Further Information—Write to: State of Maine
Environmental Improvement Commission
Augusta, Maine 04330

Relevant Bibliography Titles: 9, 18, 23, 28, 71, 95.

Maryland / Department of Juvenile Services

Nature and Purpose: The Department of Juvenile Services, established in 1966, is responsible for the development and administration of a comprehensive program for the care, treatment, and rehabilitation of delinquent youth. Primary responsibilities are divided into four broad areas: headquarters, juvenile court services, institutional services, and community and residential services. Within these areas are specific programs and support services designed to incorporate and coordinate the elements necessary for effective delivery of services.

154

Occupation Information: The Department's Headquarters staff includes administrative personnel for each of the four major areas; consultative staff for the various programs; and personnel for program planning research, personnel, training and staff development, and general fiscal matters. The staffing pattern of the juvenile court services program follows its three primary functions: intake, probation, and after-care services. Intake consultants (social workers) are assigned to specific state regions and screen all complaints. A juvenile may be placed under informal supervision for a specified period, and screening solves many cases without filing of delinquency petitions. The children placed on probation by juvenile court judges are supervised by juvenile probation workers. The probation worker deals closely not only with the child but also with his family, school, employer, other social and health agencies, and any other community sources which may aid in a satisfactory rehabilitative adjustment. Planning for a child's return to his community begins when he is committed; an after-care worker (social worker) is assigned to work closely with him, involving other staff and his family and community. The after-care worker also assists the child in returning to school or in finding employment. In the Department's correctional area, Youth Supervisors are responsible for the care, counseling, and supervision of youth in state facilities. The requirement for entry level social worker and Juvenile Probation Worker positions is a college degree. Additional years of experience and education are needed for higher grades in these classes. Beginning Youth Supervisor positions require graduation from high school. One or more years of experience is required for supervisory positions in this class. Salaries for all positions are competitive with other states. Assignments are statewide.

Further Information—Write to: Department of Juvenile Services
Personnel Office
6314 Windsor Mill Road
Baltimore, Maryland 21207

Relevant Bibliography Titles: 9, 15, 27, 30, 32, 55, 58, 67, 77.

155

Michigan / Civil Rights Commission

Nature and Purpose: The Civil Rights Commission was established in 1963 to secure the equal protection of civil rights without discrimination on the basis of religion, race, color, national origin, or age. The internal organization of the Commission is along functional lines with five major divisions: Compliance, Community Services, Administration, Public Information, and Research and Planning. The Compliance Division receives, investigates, and adjusts complaints of discrimination; and enforces the legal prohibitions against discrimination. The Community Services Division helps to organize and assist local communities to deal positively with human relations problems. The Administrative Services Division provides administrative direction and supportive services for all the divisions of the agency. The Public Information Division reports information about Commission activities and civil rights problems and progress to the people of Michigan. The Research and Planning Division gathers data and conducts research to clarify problems and to aid in planning and evaluating Commission programs.

Occupation Information: The agency's mission is carried out by a staff of approximately 250 professional and clerical employees. The largest number of employees are assigned to the central office in Detroit. Staff from the two major divisions, Compliance and Community Services, are assigned to eleven regional offices to be readily available to local communities. Two important positions in these divisions are those of the Civil Rights Representative and the Civil Rights Executive. Representatives investigate problems affecting minority groups or cases of alleged discrimination; prepare reports on findings; attempt to adjust differences between participants involving claims of discrimination; investigate incidents involving intergroup tension and recommend procedures for handling tense situations. They also gather information for research studies concerning minority groups. Civil Rights Executives direct and coordinate overall activities in regional offices or state regions. Minimum requirements for entry level positions are a college degree plus one year of related experience for Representatives and two years of related experience for Executives. Beginning salaries are $10,000 per annum for Civil Rights Representatives and $11,800 per annum for Civil Rights Executives.

Further Information—Write to:	State of Michigan Civil Rights Commission 1000 Cadillac Square Building Detroit, Michigan 48226
Relevant Bibliography Titles:	1, 8, 9, 13, 14, 24, 25, 71, 77, 95, 98.

Michigan / Department of Mental Health

Nature and Purpose:	The Michigan Department of Mental Health is responsible for providing care and treatment to the mentally ill and retarded of the state. Twenty facilities are located around the state to make services accessible to all major population centers.
Occupation Information:	A wide variety of public service careers exist in the Department of Mental Health in such areas as direct patient care, resident training, social work, and psychology. Some positions are available to people with less than a complete high school education, while others require a college degree and special training. In-service training and tuition reimbursement programs are available for staff members who wish to improve themselves. Salaries are competitive with other major employers.
Further Information—Write to:	Michigan Department of Mental Health Personnel Director Lewis Cass Building Lansing, Michigan 48926
Relevant Bibliography Titles:	9, 13, 22, 32, 57, 66, 77, 95, 110.

Michigan / Department of Natural Resources

Nature and Purpose:	It is the duty of the Michigan Department of Natural Resources to protect and conserve the state's natural resources, provide and develop facilities for outdoor recreation, prevent losses of timber and other forest values, promote reforestation of state forest lands, prevent and guard against pollution of lakes and streams,

157

enforce conservation laws, and foster the protection and reproduction of game and fish.

The Department's work takes in thousands of miles of streams,
thousands of lakes, much of the vast Great Lakes, a reservoir of
minerals, the statewide wildlife populations, and some 4.2 million
acres of state-owned lands, including 3.7 million acres of state
forests, over seventy parks, more than sixty game areas for public
hunting, and 800 public water access sites.

Occupation Information: To conduct its affairs the Department requires the services of
about 1,800 year-round employees and 450 seasonal employees.
Departmental functions in which persons usually seek career
employment include Forestry, Fisheries, Wildlife, Park Management, Outdoor Recreation, Water Resource Management, Forest Fire Control, Conservation Law Enforcement, Geology, and
Resource Planning. A brief description of some entry level positions, their requirements and beginning salaries, follow:

Conservation Aide—performs a variety of duties in the field
programs of the Forest Fire, Fisheries, or Research and Development divisions. This position requires graduation from high
school. The annual salary is $6,911.

Conservation Officer—enforces conservation laws in an assigned area and works under the direction of an Area Conservation Officer in a district. Graduation from high school is required.
The annual salary is $7,850.

Game Area Manager—serves as resident manager of dedicated
state game or wildlife areas. Requires possession of an Associate
in Science degree or its educational equivalent. The annual salary
is $7,350.

Park Ranger—does maintenance, minor construction, and enforcement work in a state park or recreation area. Graduation
from high school is required and the annual salary is $7,350.

Water Quality Investigator—makes field investigations of the
causes and extent of public water quality control problems. A
college degree or equivalent combinations of education and experience are required. The annual salary is $8,730.

On the trainee level, the following positions all require graduation from college:

Aquatic Biologist—in a water quality appraisal section, participates in surveys of lakes and streams to measure effects of industrial and municipal waste discharges on the aquatic environment.

Conservation Resource Planner—participates in the development of comprehensive and long-range plans for use of the state's
land and water resources for public use, agriculture, industry, and
recreation.

The beginning salary for these trainee positions is $9,375 per annum.

Further Information—Write to: Department of Natural Resources
Personnel Division
Stevens T. Mason Building
Lansing, Michigan 48926

Relevant Bibliography Titles: 9, 13, 14, 18, 23, 28, 71, 77, 95.

Minnesota / Department of Public Welfare

Nature and Purpose: The Department of Public Welfare is responsible for service and financial aid programs and operation of nineteen state institutions. These programs and services affect about 140,000 Minnesotans every month, including children and the institution population which averages more than 19,000 patients. People who are unable to provide for their own basic needs are helped by Public Welfare. Such assistance includes not only financial aid but social service to the aged, the mentally ill, the physically handicapped, the mentally retarded, and children and adults with special problems.

The Department is organized into an Executive unit and six Divisions: 1. Medical Services; 2. Public Assistance; 3. Child Welfare; 4. Rehabilitative Services; 5. Field Services; and 6. Administrative Services. The first four divisions constitute the Department's operating units for program supervision and services; the last two are facilitative units devoted to field liaison, accounting, and internal business management. In addition to this central office organization, the state institutions care for adults and children, and 87 county welfare boards administer the welfare programs locally.

Occupation Information: The Department of Public Welfare, because of its supervisory and consultative responsibilities, generally hires only graduate trained, experienced social workers preferably with previous experience in the area of specialization, e.g. homemaker services, unmarried parents services, foster care, etc. For the few positions where the Department does not feel the M.S.W. is necessary, they do require prior experience of their program. The Medical Services Division is headed by a psychiatrist while the Crippled

Children's Section (Rehabilitative Services Division) is headed by a pediatrician. Within the Crippled Children's Section, the Department employs Public Health Nurses (who work in an assigned territory and are headquartered within that territory), Audiologists, Speech Pathologists, and Medical Social Work Consultants. The services to the Blind Section (Rehabilitative Services Division) is responsible for services to blind clients of all ages. The majority of employees within this section are Rehabilitation Counselors who provide counseling services of all types in addition to vocational guidance. The Field Services Division has personnel headquartered out of state—individuals responsible for liaison with counties found within their assigned districts. The Administrative Services Division has Reimbursement Officers stationed within the various state hospitals for the mentally ill and the mentally retarded. In the state hospitals medical and other professional personnel are responsible for the usual types of services—dietary, nursing (patient care), rehabilitative services which include occupational, physical, and recreational therapy as well as counseling services and education, maintenance and medical. The balance of the employees of the Department perform auxiliary and clerical services. The salary ranges vary according to the type of work performed—for example, entry level nursing services (Hospital Aide) has a range of $393–$516 per month, most classes covered by the state's College Placement Examination have a range of $708–$913 per month, and Public Health Nurses start at $861 and go up to $1,134 per month.

Further Information—Write to:
State of Minnesota
Department of Public Welfare
Centennial Office Building
St. Paul, Minnesota 55101

Relevant Bibliography Titles: 9, 13, 20, 21, 27, 32, 33, 55, 57, 66, 75, 95.

Missouri / Division of Health

Nature and Purpose: The purpose of the Division of Health is the prevention of disease and the promotion of the health of the citizens of Missouri. This is achieved in many ways. One is by assisting practicing physicians in their constant effort to improve the health of Missouri's people. Another is by maintaining health education activities to assist Missourians to gain an ever-increasing awareness of their responsibility for the preservation of their own good health. A third is by minimizing possible sources of infection over which the individual has little or no control. A fourth is by maintaining quality control over services offered by institutions serving the public needs. Another is by assisting industry in meeting its requirements governing the shipment of foods and drugs in interstate commerce.

Occupation Information:

For efficiency and economy of operation the state of Missouri has been divided into five public health districts. The staff of each district serves approximately twenty-three counties. The staff consists of a health officer and public health nurses, health educators, nutritionists, sanitarians, and other public health workers. Basically, the district offices serve to support and amplify the work of local county health units. The Health Officer, a licensed physician, develops and implements public health programs in his district. They may also be assigned to local units or participate in statewide programs. The beginning salary for this position is $20,300 annually. Public Health Nurses are responsible for the educational, investigational, and community organization activities connected with the public health nursing program and, in addition, they perform nursing services in homes, schools, and clinics of the community. A Public Health Nurse I has a starting salary of $5,940 per annum. A bachelor's degree in nursing is required. Health Educators are responsible for the development and implementation of health education activities to meet the needs of the assigned area or program. This work involves extensive public contact and community organization activities as well as the preparation and dissemination of health information. Incumbents in grade I of this position must have a college degree and they begin with a yearly salary of $5,940. Nutritionists who implement programs in their field either on a local, regional, or statewide level are required to have a bachelor's degree in dietetics or a related field for beginning positions. Their annual salary is $6,540. Sanitarians, in the district offices, are responsible for promoting environmental sanitation and in enforcing sanitary rules, regulations, and ordinances. A college degree with specialization in sanitary science or an allied area is required. The beginning salary is $6,540 per annum. Other public health workers found in district or local units are Health Program Representatives, microbiologists, Public Health Dentists, Sanitary Engineers, and Speech Therapists, to name but a few.

Further Information—Write to: Division of Health of Missouri
Bureau of Personnel Services
Jefferson City, Missouri 65101

Relevant Bibliography Titles: 4, 9, 22, 32, 57, 110.

New Hampshire / Department of Employment Security

Nature and Purpose: The primary mission of the Department of Employment Security is the successful placement of individuals who are unemployed. An auxiliary responsibility is providing opportunities to change employment for those individuals who are underemployed. As a stop-gap mission the Department is also responsible for providing unemployment compensation to those unemployed individuals who qualify in accordance with the regulations established under state and federal law.

Occupation Information: To provide services to the unemployed who apply to the employment offices for assistance, the Department maintains a staff of Interviewers and Counselors who are trained in interviewing and counseling principles and techniques as implementing members in a helping profession. The Interviewers are basically responsible for referral and placement of unemployed persons, job development activities, and recognition of the need of counseling. Counselors perform in-depth interviewing for the purpose of bringing unemployed individuals to their maximum possible degee of employability. This may involve the use of personal adjustment techniques, testing of one or more types with strong emphasis on aptitude testing or assignment to an appropriate training program. Overall guidance and coordinating responsibility for the work of employment counselors is maintained throughout the state by a Chief of Counseling Services. The actual interviewing process may be conducted by an Interviewer Trainee which is the initial position in the Employment Service "helping profession" job categories. Qualifications for this position are a college degree, or an equivalent combination of education and experience. For a person initially hired as an Interviewer the requirements are a college degree and one year of experience. The entry level counseling position is that of Employment Counselor Trainee. This position requires completion of a four-year

162

college course. For those entering the Department as a Counselor the requirements are possession of a master's degree and one year of experience. The annual starting salary in the above categories are as follows: Interviewer Trainee—$6,133; Interviewer—$6,528; Counselor Trainee—$6,528; and Counselor—$7,129.

Further Information—Write to:
State of New Hampshire
Department of Employment Security
32 South Main Street
Concord, New Hampshire 03301

Relevant Bibliography Titles: 9, 13, 32, 95.

New Hampshire / Office of Economic Opportunity (SEOO)

Nature and Purpose:
The New Hampshire Office of Economic Opportunity (SEOO), formed in 1964, has three main programs: Vista Sponsorship, State Technical Assistance Program, and Conduct/Administration:

1. Vista—The SEOO, with the consent of the Governor, sponsors the VISTAS in the state of New Hampshire. There are both "National Pool" and "Community" (local low income) Volunteers. The VISTAS are assigned to Community Action Agencies which are delegate agencies and are responsible for supervision of the Volunteers working on projects.

2. State Technical Assistance Program (STAP) is for delivery of technical assistance to Community Action Agencies in a long-term, concentrated manner. There are three areas of expertise—housing, manpower, and economic development.

3. Conduct and Administration: The Director is appointed by the Governor with consent of the Executive Council. He is adviser of the Governor and OEO, liaison for CAAS with the state, advocate of the poor and responsible for function of the office and SEOO programs.

Occupation Information:
The following personnel help carry out the agency's mission: VISTA Program Analysts on the SEOO staff overlook VISTA in the state. A baccalaureate degree and previous VISTA experience is required. While incumbents are based in Concord, New Hampshire, there is 50 percent in-state travel and 20 percent out-of-

163

state travel. Since the program is a yearly contract with VISTA, service is a year at a time. STAP Specialists are outstationed with CAAS and receive a contract rather than a salary. The Specialist must have a baccalaureate degree, expertise in the specific area, and experience working with the poor. Service is year to year. Training Specialists coordinate all training and technical assistance to OEO grantees within the state as well as monitoring all training. Teacher training is required as well as experience working with the poor. Grant Specialists in SEOO supervise the technical aspects and preparation of all SEOO grants and give technical assistance to CAAS on grantsmanship. They also serve as manpower specialists and give training and technical assistance to grantees in manpower. They must be expert in math, and have a thorough knowledge of grantsmanship and manpower programs. A college degree is preferred, but may be waived for experience. Program Coordinators act as contacts for grantees and the SEOO; they serve as liaison with state, local, and federal agencies for grantees and low income groups. They also act as coordinators for Head Start. Program Coordinators must have a baccalaureate degree and experience working with the disadvantaged. Salaries, for all these positions, are dependent upon experience and qualifications.

Further Information—Write to:

Director
New Hampshire Office of Economic Opportunity
15 North Main Street
Concord, New Hampshire 03301

Relevant Bibliography Titles: 9, 13, 71, 94, 95, 104.

New Jersey / Department of Labor and Industry

Nature and Purpose:

Major divisions within the Department of Labor and Industry are: The Division of Unemployment Disability Insurance which administers the state's disability insurance program, providing cash benefits to specific classes of employees disabled by non-occupational sickness or accident; the Office of Manpower Program which administers the Work Incentive Program, Employment Services, Manpower Training Programs, Rehabilitation Services, and develops specialized research programs to improve and extend vocational rehabilitation services to handicapped people; and the Division of Labor and Standards which administers, through its three Bureaus, occupational safety regulations, major laws dealing with wages, hours and working conditions, and statutes providing for the health, safety, and welfare of migrant workers.

Occupation Information: The Department employs personnel with varied academic and experience backgrounds to fulfill its various responsibilities. Brief descriptions of relevant positions within the agency, giving requirements and salaries, follow.

To help unemployed and disadvantaged Spanish-speaking people, special Community Employment Service Workers assist professional staff in implementing programs whose aim is the training and employment of these people. Requirements for this position are graduation from high school and three years of experience in dealing with disadvantaged youth and adults. The annual entry level salary is $7,090. Employment services are also provided by Employment Counselors and Rehabilitation Counselors. The former provides specialized employment counseling to applicants who present occupational problems of choice, change, or adjustment; the latter locates and makes investigations of disabled persons in need of vocational rehabilitation, determines their eligibility for services, makes arrangements for the provision of physical restoration services, and through counseling and guidance assists such persons in selecting, preparing for, and attaining the vocational adjustment affording the greatest social and economic satisfaction. Both positions require college degrees and one year of related experience; the beginning annual salary is $9,045.

The staff responsible for administering various safety laws and regulations include: Safety Engineers who examine engineering plans, and make investigations to determine compliance with occupational safety and health rulings; Safety Inspectors who investigate structural conditions of buildings and examine equipment used to protect lives and insure safety of workers; Construction Safety Inspectors who, in turn, inspect all construction and demolition projects to enforce compliance; inspection of quarries and excavations to insure that workers' health and safety are not endangered is the responsibility of the Explosives Safety Inspector; and inspections of mines, mining operations, and quarries are carried out by Mining Safety Inspectors. All positions require graduation from high school except for Safety Engineers who must have a college degree. Varying amounts of related experience are required for all classes. Engineers begin at $10,470 per annum; the other positions have a beginning salary of $7,800 per annum.

In the area of migrant labor, Inspectors visit camps and tenant houses in an assigned district, occupied by migrant agricultural or industrial workers and make inspections of housing and sanitary conditions. They report violations of the law and prepare reports on each assignment. Requirements for this position include graduation from high school and two years of experience. $6,750 is the annual starting salary.

Assignments, for all of the above positions, can be in any of the more than 200 field offices of the Department scattered throughout the state.

Further Information—Write to:

Department of Labor and Industry
Office of Personnel and Training
John Fitch Plaza, Room 1213
Trenton, New Jersey 08625

Relevant Bibliography Titles: 9, 13, 43, 65, 71, 74, 94, 95.

New York / Department of Environmental Conservation

Nature and Purpose:

The Department of Environmental Conservation has wide responsibilities for the land, waters, air, fish, and wildlife, and other resources which are the environment of the citizens of New York State. The goal of the Department is to enhance the quality of life in New York State. To meet this goal the Department carries out programs to: prevent water, air, land, and noise pollution; control the use of pesticides harmful to man, animal, and plant life; regulates the storage, handling, and transportation of solids, liquids, and gases to prevent pollution; manage and protect fish and wildlife; protect and administer the forest preserve; promote the restoration and reclamation of despoiled areas; conserve agricultural land, river valleys, open lands, and other areas. In addition, the Department establishes environmental standards and coordinates and enforces the environmental policy of the state and develops environmental plans for the future.

Occupation Information:

The functions of the Department are carried out by a staff of administrative and professional personnel. Brief descriptions follow of the various relevant positions found within the Department's major Divisions.

The Division of Lands and Forests employs Foresters, Forest

166

Rangers, and Forestry Technicians. Foresters work on forest nursery operations and forest management and protection; they prepare management plans, advise on marketing and reforestation, negotiate for purchase of land, prepare forestry exhibits, and give public talks. A bachelor's degree in forestry is required. The annual salary ranges from $8,648 to $10,104. Trainees in this position begin at $8,169 per annum. The duties of Forest Rangers, in this Division, covers fire suppression, law enforcement, and protection of state land. Ranger School graduation or its equivalent is required; the salary range is $6,575 to $8,105. Among the Division's support staff are Forestry Technicians who conduct field work in forest insect and disease control including the supervision of seasonal laborers engaged in scouting or eradication work. Ranger School graduation or its equivalent is required. The entry level salary is $5,546 per annum.

Conservation Biologists and Conservation Officers are employed by the Division of Fish and Wildlife. Biologists, depending on Bureau assignment, do research and experimental work relating to fish resources and assist in testing and making recommendations for fish management programs and methods; or they may carry out game research investigations and direct wildlife research and management projects. Requirements include a bachelor's degree in fisheries, wildlife, natural resources, or closely related management or research fields. The annual salary range for biologists is $8,648 to $10,104. Trainees begin at $8,169. The Conservation Officer enforces the New York State Fish and Wildlife Law. They must have a thorough knowledge of the fish and wildlife in the territory where their job is located. Their salary range is $6,575 to $8,105.

The Division of Water Resources acts as the operating staff for the Water Resources Commission. It is concerned primarily with regulation of the use of the state's water resources and the formulation of comprehensive long-range plans to insure optimum development of these resources. Positions consist largely of hydraulic engineers, economists, and clerical personnel.

Personnel in the Environmental Quality Division are responsible for administering and carrying out air, water, and related environmental quality control activities. With few exceptions, all positions require either a four-year degree in engineering or scientific specialty, or a two-year degree in engineering technology.

Further Information—Write to: State of New York
Department of Environmental Conservation
Albany, New York 12201

Relevant Bibliography Titles: 9, 13, 18, 23, 28, 95.

New York / Narcotic Addiction Control Commission (NACC)

Nature and Purpose:

The Narcotic Addiction Control Commission was established in 1971 to mount an attack on the problem of narcotic addiction and drug abuse. The Commission has full responsibility for developing and operating services and facilities in the areas of prevention, treatment and rehabilitation, and research.

When addiction is proven, an addict is committed to the Narcotic Addiction Control Commission, which then makes an assignment to the treatment and rehabilitation program where efforts are tailored to meet the individual's needs. There is no one "state answer" to the problem, and rehabilitation may consist of detoxification, physical and mental build-up, counseling services, on-going team evaluation, and, when therapeutically indicated, specialized treatment such as drug maintenance. When the addict has made sufficient progress, he becomes part of the NACC aftercare program which includes: a field service, providing rehabilitants with counseling and guidance; a residential center, serving as a halfway house; and a day care center, providing rehabilitants with vocational training, academic tutoring, medical services, and recreational activities.

Occupation Information:

The Narcotic Addiction Control Commission's staff is composed of personnel with greatly varied educational backgrounds. In the areas of rehabilitation and research there are career opportunities for nurses, psychiatrists, clinical physicians, psychologists, teachers, dieticians, dentists, dental hygienists, and many others. Two important positions in Rehabilitation Centers are those of the Narcotic Rehabilitation Counselor and the Narcotic Correction Officer. The Narcotic Rehabilitation Counselor supervises and guides residents in the rehabilitation center. They are responsible for a multi-disciplinary rehabilitative treatment program in the rehabilitation center, where they work on a team with psychologists, psychiatrists, educators, recreationists, and ward service personnel. They also provide group and individual therapy as needed, counseling patients on their adjustments to community life, families, jobs, and other personal affairs. Qualifications include a bachelor's degree and one year of counseling experience.

The annual entry level salary is $11,470. Narcotic Correction Officers are responsible for the welfare and the continuing therapeutic program of the patients on their wards. They participate in individual and group counseling sessions; in recreational activity programs; and in vocational and educational training and retraining. Graduation from high school is required for this position. The entry level salary is $6,535 per annum. In the area of narcotic aftercare the Commission has a staff of Narcotic Parole Officers who supervise and guide rehabilitants in the aftercare program. They help each find a suitable job and living quarters; determine whether he has remained free of drug dependency; recommend changes in his program; and prepare case reports. Narcotic Parole Officers must be either graduates from law school or college graduates with two years of related experience. The entry level annual salary is $12,100. In the educational area of the Commission's program a relevant position is that of the Community Narcotic Education Representative. This staff member divides his time between the storefront centers, community speaking engagements, and organizational efforts in order to explain the Commission's treatment and rehabilitation program to individuals and community groups. A bachelor's degree and one year of experience in a related field are required; the beginning salary is $6,965 per annum. Assignments, for all positions described above, are at various NACC centers and facilities throughout New York State.

Further Information—Write to: Narcotic Addiction Control Commission
Office of Employee Relations
Executive Park South
Stuyvesant Plaza
Albany, New York 12203

Relevant Bibliography Titles: 9, 10, 13, 23, 32, 34, 66, 67, 71, 110.

North Carolina / State Board of Health

Nature and Purpose: The State Board of Health is charged with the responsibility of public health in North Carolina. Health programs are delivered primarily at the community level through the facility of local health departments. The programs that are made available vary from multiphasic screening, glaucoma clinic, cancer clinic, crippled children, maternal and child health, home health agencies, and several others.

Occupation Information: The Board's responsibility is met by the utilization of many various medical and administrative disciplines. In the area of administration, there is a classification referred to as the Health Administrator. These non-medical, discipline administrators have a background in public health and handle the administrative aspects of delivering a medical program. Minimum qualifications for this class includes a master's degree in public health, and two years of experience in administrative management work related to a health program. Salaries range from $11,340 for Health Administrator I to $19,235 for Health Administrator V. Also on the State Board of Health's staff are medical consultants with which these nonmedical administrators confer. The various consultants also provide interpretation, guidance, and assistance to their counterpart within the local health departments. A Public Health Nursing Consultant, for example, serves as a consultant in assisting the development and extension of a generalized public health nursing program in local health departments or in a specialized field such as maternal and child health, mental health, crippled children, occupational health, and pediatrics. Requirements for entry level positions in this class include completion of a program of study accredited by the National League for Nursing for public health nursing, a master's degree in nursing or public health and two years of nursing experience; the beginning annual salary is $8,170. Other personnel found in state and local health units include; public health educators; dentists; dental assistants; doctors, nurses; nutritionists, public health dietitians; and physical therapists. In the area of communicable diseases local departments also employ Public Health Investigators. Employees in this class apply case-finding and educational techniques in working with individuals having venereal disease and other communicable or chronic diseases. A college degree is required for this position; and the beginning salary is $7,165 per annum. In the health engineering field Industrial Hygiene Technicians and Engineers conduct investigations for the state occupational health protection programs. Sanitary Engineers and technicians are concerned with statewide programs in pollution abatement, water quality, and insect and rodent control. Programs concerned wih the control of air pollution employ Air Hygienists who are responsible for coordinating technical support of engineers, sanitarians, and other professional personnel. Positions in the health engineering field require a minimum of graduation from college with major study in an applicable area. Salaries range from

170

$7,160 to $15,100 per annum depending on education and experience. Assignments are statewide, in either state or local health units.

Further Information—Write to:

North Carolina
State Board of Health
P.O. Box 2091
Raleigh, North Carolina 27602

Relevant Bibliography Titles:

4, 9, 22, 23, 32, 57, 95, 110.

Ohio / Department of Development / Community Economic Improvement Group (CEIG)

Nature and Purpose:

The Community Economic Improvement Group (CEIG) is a new state agency within the Department of Development created to improve the economic conditions of the economically disadvantaged communities throughout the state of Ohio. The CEIG has developed various programs to fulfill this mission. The following represents a partial listing of these programs.

(1) "Universities" Project: A task force, having representatives from a broad sample of universities and community development corporations across the state, has been assembled for the purpose of designating a statewide system of college and university extension to assist the economic development of depressed areas in Ohio.

(2) Contract Procurement for Minorities: In conjunction with several other state agencies, CEIG has arranged a series of workshops for minority entrepreneurs in six major Ohio cities.

(3) State Minority Business Directory: The CEIG is gathering data for the purpose of publishing a State Minority Business Directory. The Directory will include information concerning identification, capability, goods or services provided, owners' experience, educational background, length of time in business, number of employees, capitalization, and annual receipts.

(4) S.O.M.B. (Selling Opportunities for Minority Business): This program deals primarily with contract procurement for minority businesses. It covers federal and state government contract opportunities as well as subcontracting with major businesses.

171

Occupation Information: Professional staff employees of CEIG are required to have experience or educational background in business, economics, city and regional planning, or other related areas. All employees presently work in the Ohio Department building, but the scope of the CEIG is statewide. Salaries are commensurate with other departments of the state.

Further Information—Write to: Director
Community Economic Improvement Group
Room 1012—65 South Front Street
Columbus, Ohio 43215

Relevant Bibliography Titles: 9, 13, 71, 81, 82, 94, 95.

Oklahoma / State Department of Health

Nature and Purpose: The State Department of Health, established in 1890, is directly responsible for the administration of legislative acts dealing with public health in Oklahoma. The Department receives and disburses to local health departments and other health agencies funds allocated by the state and the U.S. Congress for most public health programs. The public health services provided are in environmental health, community health, mental, maternal and child health, personal health, statistics, laboratory and health facilities. Organized programs emphasize prevention, early detection, and abatement of disease. In addition, the State Department of Health supervises operation of the Eastern Oklahoma Tuberculosis Sanatorium in Talihina, the Western Oklahoma Tuberculosis Sanitorium, and Oklahoma General Hospital, both in Clinton.

The State Department of Health has six Line Services: Mental Health and Maternal and Child Health Services; Community Health Services; Environmental Health Services; Communicable Disease Control and Laboratory Services; Health Facilities Services; and Personal Health Services. These Services deliver public health programs to people and institutions, both directly and through local health departments.

Occupation Information: Public health services are organized into programs which are delivered by qualified people in the community, county, state, and national settings. There are approximately 1,000 state and local public health workers in Oklahoma. Many of the positions in the state and the fifty-nine county health departments offer the opportunity for work with health related social and emotional problems as well as the whole gamut of environmental situations. The following program areas are those in which personnel are most involved in reaching out to help people: Maternal and Child Health, Mental Health Guidance Services, Family Planning, and Nursing Services.

The Maternal and Child Health program provides health supervision of mothers and children. Two types of positions with outreach are found within this program—Public Health Nurse and Licensed Practical Nurse. Minimum requirements for the former is an R.N. and for the latter is a license. Entry level monthly salaries are $550 for Public Health Nurses and $415 for Licensed Practical Nurses. Assignments are in Child Health Conferences, clinics, and in the community.

The Mental Health Guidance Services program provides mental health-public health services; and, in addition, provides evaluation and counseling for children, parents, and the community. Three types of relevant positions exist within this program—Psychologist, Social Worker, and Child Development Specialist. All positions require a master's degree. The beginning salaries for the first two are $685 per month. The Child Development Specialist has a monthly salary of $645. Assignments are in regional and county Guidance Clinics.

The Family Planning program provides clinic and recruitment services for women desiring to limit their family size. Social Workers, Public Health Community Workers, and Neighborhood Health Visitors are some of the relevant personnel utilized in this program. Public Health Community Workers, who must be high school graduates and have some previous experience, assist in publicizing and implementing the maternity and family planning service. They also help coordinate the volunteer program augmenting the clinic's services. Their beginning salary is $370 per month. It is the responsibility of the Neighborhood Health Visitor to interpret the program to the community and to encourage residents to avail themselves of these services. The only requirements for this position are the ability to read and write the English language and residence in the target area. The beginning monthly salary is $330. Assignments are in Family Planning Clinics.

The Home Health Care program provides intermittent care of the ill or disabled person in his home through Public Health Nurses, Licensed Practical Nurses, and Home Health Aides. While the two classes of Nurses perform various levels of professional nursing services, the Home Health Aides perform those supportive services which are required to provide and maintain normal bodily and emotional comfort and they assist the home-bound patient toward independent living in a safe environment. The ability to read and write and successful completion of a special training course is required for Aides. The beginning salary is $330 per month. Personnel are assigned to the home's of patients.

Further Information—Write to: Oklahoma State Department of Health
3400 N. Eastern
Oklahoma City, Oklahoma 73105

Relevant Bibliography Titles: 9, 13, 22, 32, 55, 57, 66, 95, 110.

Pennsylvania / Department of Community Affairs

Nature and Purpose: The Department of Community Affairs was created in 1966. Its basic functions are to help solve urban and community problems and to create better communities throughout Pennsylvania.

Occupation Information: The following brief descriptions are of career positions that exist within the Department for imaginative community-conscious people.

Community Research Analyst positions involve work in the field of local government and the related programs of the Department. Analysts conduct research studies on a full range of local government activities and analyze and evaluate departmental programs. This work involves frequent contact with state and local officials.

Human Resources Development Specialist positions involve administrative work in a staff capacity assisting in the state economic development program, analyzing and evaluating programs developed by communities and state agencies. This work includes the preparation of applications for federal approval of programs involving health, welfare, employment, or education services. Employees in these positions mobilize human and economic resources to aid deprived citizens in achieving their full social and economic potential.

Housing and Redevelopment Analyst positions require varying degrees of expertise in housing and community development. Analysts supervise, analyze, and report on programs directed at

174

improving urban and rural environmental conditions, reviewing and evaluating proposals for projects, and consulting with local government officials in promoting sound redevelopment and planning principles.

Community Services Consultants provide a variety of specialized, technical consulting services to local government officials to help communities organize or improve operations in either public safety, finance, public works, codes administration, government organization, intergovernmental relations, and general administration.

Planning Analysts are engaged in professional planning and administrative work at the local, regional, or state level coordinating the state's local planning assistance program, and assisting in the development of local and regional planning programs.

Recreation & Parks Advisers provide technical and professional assistance to local government officials in recreation, parks, and conservation planning, development, and administration, to increase the quality and quantity of local governmental recreation programs and facilities.

Requirements for all these positions, at the entry level, include a bachelor's degree and one or more years of related experience. The beginning salary is $9,011 per annum.

Further Information—Write to: Department of Community Affairs
Personnel Officer
Harrisburg, Pennsylvania 17120

Relevant Bibliography Titles: 9, 13, 71, 82, 94, 104.

South Carolina / State Board of Health / Family Planning Program

Nature and Purpose: Family planning services are offered in all 46 county health departments of South Carolina. The major objectives of the program are: to offer quality family planning services to all in South Carolina who need and desire the service without regard to color, creed, religion, sex, length of residence, or marital status; and to operate a coordinated state program of family planning that provides for cooperation between all public and private agencies and groups involved with and interested in family planning in South Carolina.

175

Occupation Information:

In addition to a supporting clerical staff, the following personnel implement the family planning program on the state and district levels: health officers, coordinators, nurses, social workers, physicians, and outreach workers. Outreach workers, called Community Health Aides, make home visits to potential family planning patients. Most of the home visits are made to those who have been referred to the program for family planning. Outreach also consists of aides making talks to community groups to interest them in family planning. The aides also visit those prenatal patients identified as high risk to interest them in family planning. Whenever possible, outreach workers are recruited from the community to be served. They are required to have an eighth grade education and their beginning annual salary is $3,430. All other staff members must have educational backgrounds commensurate with the responsibilities of their positions. Medical Social Workers, for instance, must have a master's degree in social work; their annual salary begins at $7,600. Consultant positions in nursing or medical social work require progressively more years of related experience and carry higher beginning salaries as the area of responsibility increases. All new staff personnel undergo extensive training in family planning services. This training is organized and in part provided by state-level family planning staff. Assignments are statewide.

Further Information—Write to:

South Carolina State Board of Health
Personnel Director
J. Marion Sims Building
Columbia, South Carolina 29201

Relevant Bibliography Titles:

9, 13, 26, 32, 49, 55, 57, 77, 95.

South Carolina / State Department of Public Welfare

Nature and Purpose:

The State Department of Public Welfare is responsible for the administration of Aid to the Aged, Aid to the Blind, Aid to Dependent Children, and assistance to other handicapped and unfortunate persons. In addition, the Department administers state institutions which have been established to care for those in need of special services.

Occupation Information: A wide range of administrative, professional, and nontechnical personnel carry out the Department's mission. The following selected positions exist within each of the Department's forty-six county welfare offices: homemaker; caseworker; medical social worker; and county welfare director. The Director is responsible for the overall operation of the office; and he administers the funds for public assistance, child welfare, and services for the blind. Direct social services to individuals and families are given by Caseworkers and Medical Social Workers. In-home help to families in emergencies and stress is given by the Homemaker who tries to maintain a family's normal way of living or tries to help them improve their living conditions. The professional positions in this series require graduation from college. Additional years of experience are needed for more responsible assignments. Annual salaries range from $6,120 for beginning Caseworkers to $10,200 for experienced Welfare County Directors. Homemakers, a nonprofessional position, must have an eighth grade education; their annual salary begins at $3,430. All employees participate in some type of training related to their area of employment. Assignments are allocated to each of the county offices located throughout the state.

Further Information—Write to: State Department of Public Welfare
P.O. Box 1520
Columbia, South Carolina 29202

Relevant Bibliography Titles: 9, 13, 21, 29, 32, 41, 55, 75, 95.

Texas / State Commission for the Blind

Nature and Purpose: The State Commission for the Blind was established in 1931. In the early years of its operation it administered only state-funded services which were restricted to legally or totally blind persons. About 1945 the agency began to provide federally-funded rehabilitation services to blind adults. Eye medical services for children were maintained as a state-funded service and still are. Since 1965 there has been an expansion of services and personnel to deliver a wide range of services. A variety of three-party agreements are operational so that there are such unusual programs, administered by the State Commission for the Blind, as services to blind MH-MR clients in institutional settings; a Business Enterprise Program; and a number of special projects operating, such as: services to clients in penal institutions; services for patients dismissed from state hospitals or mentally retarded clients who are on waiting lists for admission to special schools; and the Criss Cole Rehabilitation Center—a personal adjustment center. A division of technical and consultative services supervises and coordinates visually-handicapped children's caseworkers consultant services, rehabilitation teacher consultant services, facilities consultant services, and staff development.

Occupation Information: The Commission's present-day program encompasses rehabilitation services delivered to visually-impaired as well as legally and totally blind clients through a team composed of a Rehabilitation Counselor, Rehabilitation Teacher, and Placement Specialist. Personnel in these positions are required to have either a bachelor's degree or a master's degree. Rehabilitation Counselor and Placement Specialist salaries start at $10,000. Entry level Rehabilitation Teachers earn $7,000 per annum. Other relevant positions within the Commission are those for Rehabilitation Technicians, Business Enterprise Program Supervisors; and Visually-Handicapped Children's Caseworkers. These positions all require graduation from college, and have a beginning annual salary of $7,000. In-service training and staff development are provided to all personnel. Assignments are statewide since there are twenty-one district offices and several special projects.

Further Information—Write to: State Commission for the Blind
Personnel Officer
P.O. Box 12866
Austin, Texas 78711

Relevant Bibliography Titles: 9, 13, 21, 30, 32, 33, 55, 57, 77, 95, 110.

Texas / Texas Rehabilitation Commission

Nature and Purpose: It is the responsibility of the Texas Rehabilitation Commission to provide handicapped citizens with services that will enable them to enter or return to gainful employment. It also processes claims for cash disability benefits under the federal Social Security Act. The state-federal vocational rehabilitation program today provides services to citizens with mental retardation, mental illness, behavioral disorder (including alcoholism, drug addiction and both adult and youthful public offenders), amputations and other orthopedic impairments, speech and hearing disorders, deafness, heart disorders, epilepsy, cancer, stroke, tuberculosis, congenital deformities and neurological disabilities, and other disabling conditions.

Occupation Information: Two important staff members, within the Texas Rehabilitation Commission, are the Rehabilitation Technician and the Vocational Rehabilitation Counselor. Together with other staff members of a professional team, which includes nurses, doctors, and therapists, they assist handicapped clients to become rehabilitated. The Rehabilitation Technician and the Vocational Rehabilitation Counselor assist and guide handicapped persons and their families so that they can deal with the problem with which the handicapped person is confronted, select a proper vocational goal, and make plans to reach it. Technicians, concerned with less complex case services, are required to have two years of college and, in addition, one year of experience. The entry level annual salary is $7,560. Counselors, who are responsible for caseloads dealing with complex disabilities, are required to have a master's degree or a college degree with two years of related experience. Entry level Vocational Rehabilitation Counselors have a beginning annual salary of $10,175. There is a staff training period of approximately twelve months for Technicians and Counselors. Assignments are at any of 200 locations throughout the state.

Further Information—Write to: Texas Rehabilitation Commission
Personnel Office
1301 East 38th Street
Austin, Texas 78705

179

Relevant Bibliography Titles: 9, 13, 21, 30, 32, 33, 57, 65, 66, 95.

Vermont / Department of Mental Health

Nature and Purpose: The Vermont Department of Mental Health administers eleven Community Mental Health Agencies, the Brattleboro Retreat, the Brandon Training School, and the Vermont State Hospital. The eleven Community Mental Health Agencies provide services throughout the state. Each of these services has three program levels: (1) direct treatment services for the mentally ill and retarded; (2) indirect consultation services to community health, welfare, educational and other social resources; and (3) preventive services. The Vermont State Hospital provides immediate, intensive treatment services to Vermont citizens to alleviate acute mental illness and counteract tendencies toward chronicity and invalidism. The Hospital is organized to provide a concentration of a variety of highly trained treatment professionals and treatment facilities on a 24-hour basis. The initial objective of the Vermont State Hospital is to restore the patient to the level of health and function that will allow him to leave the Hospital to continue his convalescence elsewhere.

Occupation Information: There are career opportunities within the Department of Mental Health for anyone with an interest in people. Community Mental Health Centers employ social workers, psychologists, nutrition aides, nurses, and other professional and technical personnel. The Vermont State Hospital employs everyone from ex-patients to executives. Aides usually engage in training programs at the hospital. There is room in the institutional system for individuals with only a high school education as well as those with Ph.D.'s. There are also positions for Foster Grandparents at the Brandon Training School, so that people over sixty-five have a chance to feel responsible and have an income again. Positions in the Community Mental Health Centers are more flexible but higher educational degrees are required.

Further Information—Write to: State of Vermont
Department of Mental Health
State Office Building
Montpelier, Vermont 05602

State Agencies

Relevant Bibliography Titles: 9, 13, 22, 32, 66, 95.

Virginia / Department of Conservation and Economic Development

Nature and Purpose:

The Department of Conservation and Economic Development is concerned with environmental maintenance and improvement. It is charged by law with responsibility for promotion of tree planting, determination of the best uses of water, land and forest resources, and administration of the state parks and recreation areas.

Occupation Information:

The Department has career opportunities which utilize many specialized skills. Many of these positions require college degrees in forestry, silviculture, geology, and water engineering, while other positions require lesser education and experience. The state parks and recreation areas need special supervision by those familiar with conservation and public relations. The following personnel are employed to carry out some of the various functions of the Department:

State Park Chief Ranger—performs and supervises buildings and grounds maintenance and housekeeping services in a state-owned recreational park. Requirements for this position include graduation from high school or an equivalent education, and one year of experience in building maintenance or work as a trades helper. The beginning salary is $5,640 per annum.

State Park Superintendent—supervises the operation and maintenance of a state-owned park or recreation area. Requirements include high school graduation and three years of experience one of which must be as a Chief Ranger. $7,030 is the beginning salary.

Forest Warden—supervises and organizes forest fire control and prevention, enforces forest fire laws, and assists in forest management and reforestation work in an assigned area comprising one or two counties, organizes and trains fire crews at high schools and in communities; and gives forest conservation talks to school children and adults. Requirements include completion of high school and two years of experience in forest fire control work. The beginning salary is $5,640 per annum.

Supporting these personnel are Forestry Aides and Assistants who assist in forest fire suppression activities and various other

181

areas of forestry work. These positions require less education and experience and entry level salaries range from $4,320 to $4,920 per annum.

Further Information—Write to: Department of Conservation and Economic Development
1100 State Office Building
Richmond, Virginia 23219

Relevant Bibliography Titles: 9, 13, 18, 23, 28, 95.

Virginia / Division of State Planning and Community Affairs

Nature and Purpose: The Division of State Planning and Community Affairs is one of seven divisions under the Governor's Office of Administration. Originally part of the Division of Industrial Development and Planning, the Division of Planning was created in 1966 and it acquired its present name and functions in 1968. The Division encourages, assists, and coordinates the planning efforts of state agencies, governmental subdivisions, and planning districts. In addition, the Division assumes responsibility for a number of special research activities as required by legislative study commissions. Through its eleven operating sections, the Division provides a variety of professional and technical services in fulfilling its responsibilities.

Occupation Information: The Division of State Planning and Community Affairs offers a wide range of career opportunities for individuals interested in human resources and community planning at the state government level. Two positions basic to the functions and mission of the Division are those of the State Planning Assistant and the State Planner. State Planning Assistants assist professional planners or administrators by collecting, organizing, and presenting resource data related to existing or proposed programs of a regionalized or statewide scope. The work involves gathering information required as part of comprehensive studies of past and present practices and conditions in an assigned program or geographical area. Brief or extended visits are made to localities to interview public officials and private citizens, inspect records, and observe firsthand the conditions of life or the effects of existing programs in the area. Flexibility of approach is a continuing requirement

182

as incumbents are moved to assignments of varying nature and scope. Examples of the types of studies to which assignments may be made include human services delivery systems, old age planning, model cities assistance, program planning activities, and environmental protection studies. Requirements for this position include a bachelor's degree with major studies in planning, the social sciences, or a related field, and one year of experience. The beginning salary is $7,680 per annum. Performing increasingly more complex and responsible duties in this area are State Planners who conduct studies and develop plans for the revision or replacement of programs, the mobilization of human or economic resources, and the satisfaction of short and long term needs and objectives. A master's degree in planning, public administration, or a related field and one year of experience are required. State Planners begin at a salary of $10,032 per annum.

Further Information—Write to:

Commonwealth of Virginia
Division of State Planning and Community Affairs
1010 James Monroe Building
109 Governor Street
Richmond, Virginia 23219

Relevant Bibliography Titles:

9, 71, 82, 94, 95.

Washington / Department of Natural Resources

Nature and Purpose:

Responsibilities of the Department of Natural Resources include: management of the 3,000,000 acres of state-owned land including 2,000,000 acres of forest land and 1,000,000 acres of wheat, grazing, and general agricultural land; regulates activities on 12,-300,000 acres of state and privately owned forest lands in the administration of the Forest Practices Act; advises farmers and small woodlot owners regarding management of their forest lands through the Farm Forestry program; protects about 12,3000,000 acres of state and privately owned forest lands from forest fires, insects, and diseases; and provides governmental services, conducts research and administers laws pertaining to mines, geology, timber production, and management of other natural resources.

Occupation Information:

The Department's staff is composed of about 850 permanent and 1,200 seasonal employees. Three hundred and fifty of the perma-

183

nent employees are in professional classifications. All positions, including subordinate to Supervisor of Natural Resources, are occupied by personnel selected for their professional training, experience, and ability to assume increasing responsibility. Career opportunities for professional employees are usually limited to entry-grade positions. The exception occurs when special preparation (usually graduate level study) is required. The beginning Forester with a B.S. degree and major study in forest management starts as a Forester I. Usually, the Forester I is offered a position with a working title and duties as follows:

Management Forester—works under the direct supervision of a Forester II in all phases of forest management work involving state-owned lands. This may include cruising timber, marking thinnings and sale boundaries, road locations, scaling, sales compliance, supervising planting crews, and seedling operations.

Forest Practices Forester—administers Forest Practices Act requiring that an adequate seed source be left on any state or privately owned forest lands scheduled for logging. He recommends seed source location, estimates volume logged by species and age class and makes reproduction surveys.

Inventory Forester—collects, interprets, and assembles resource inventory data, mainly by use of permanent sample plots. The work involves the location, marking, and measuring of sample plots. Aerial photos are used as well as extensive past inventory records. Specialized surveys, pertaining to reforestation, insect, disease, and fire damage are accomplished.

The beginning Engineer with a B.S. degree and a major study in forest engineering (logging engineering) or civil engineering starts as a Forest Engineer I, or as a Civil Engineer I (land survey). The duties are as follows:

Forest Engineer—locates, stakes, and designs forest roads and structures; supervises construction; and accomplishes surveying to locate property lines.

Land Surveyor—works as instrumentman on four-man survey party, accomplishing third order surveying and marking property lines. He may also work in the office computing and drafting, or checking other work associated with property line surveying.

Further Information—Write to: Commissioner of Public Lands
Department of Natural Resources
P.O. Box 168
Olympia, Washington 98501

Relevant Bibliography Titles: 9, 13, 18, 23, 28, 95.

West Virginia / Department of Welfare

Nature and Purpose:
The West Virginia Department of Welfare's program is a state-administered program, including the usual federal categories of welfare described in the Welfare Title of the Social Security Act, such as Aid to Dependent Children. The Department is also responsible for distribution of surplus food and food stamps, which is a joint operation between the Department of Health, Education, and Welfare/Department of Agriculture and the state agency. In addition, the Department administers emergency and general relief, which are county responsibilities in most other states.

Occupation Information:
The Department's usual or average personnel payroll includes in excess of 1,800 job slots, ranging from a Clerk I, at pay grade #2, $295 per month, upward through pay grade #19, the Commissioner, at $1,915 monthly. The main bulk of the Department's work, however, is accomplished through Social Service Workers and Eligibility Specialists classified from I through IV, according to their level of education and experience. An Eligibility Specialist I can qualify for employment after graduation from high school. A Social Service Worker I must have completed a minimum of sixty semester hours of college. Eligibility Specialist salaries range from a low of $330 monthly to a high of $745 monthly for Eligibility Specialist III, with seven years of experience.

Further Information—Write to:
West Virginia
Department of Welfare
Charleston, West Virginia 25305

Relevant Bibliography Titles:
9, 13, 32, 55, 75, 95.

West Virginia / Economic Opportunity Office

Nature and Purpose:
The West Virginia Economic Opportunity Office is funded to provide technical assistance to Community Action Agencies and communities not funded but desiring work with low-income peo-

ple. The Office is also funded to work with other state agencies to make sure that they are trying to keep in mind the needs of low-income people as they formulate relevant programs. The Office also operates additional programs funded by the Department of Labor and the Appalachian Regional Commission.

Occupation Information: Requirements for the various Economic Opportunity Specialist positions in the agency include completion of a four-year college program in addition to some work experience in community development or working with an OEO related project. Training is given as part of the program. Salaries range from $635 per month to $1,000 per month, depending on education and experience.

Further Information—Write to: West Virginia Economic Opportunity Office
1703 Quarrier Street
Charleston, West Virginia 25311

Relevant Bibliography Titles: 9, 13, 71, 94, 95, 104.

PART IV

Bibliography

1. ADAMS, A. JOHN, and Joan Martin Burke. *Civil Rights: A Current Guide to the People, Organizations, and Events.* New York: R. R. Bowker, 1970.
2. *Africa-Technical Assistance Programs of U.S. Non-Profit Organizations.* Ed. Jackie Horn. New York: Technical Assistance Information Clearing House, 1969.
3. *American Agencies Interested in International Affairs.* Compiled by Donald Wasson. New York: Praeger, 1964.
4. *American Medical Association Directory of National Voluntary Health Organizations—1971 Edition.* Chicago: American Medical Association, 1971.
   Contains information on the key personnel, purposes, organizational structure, financing, and program activities of some fifty national voluntary health agencies.
5. ANGEL, JUVENAL LONDOÑO. *Modern Vocational Trends Reference Handbook.* 7th ed. New York: Simon and Schuster, 1970.
   A handbook of occupational information that relates to careers for which there are expanding opportunities, and high personnel demand.
6. ————. *Selective Guide to Overseas Employment.* New York: Regents Publishing Co., 1968.
   See: Chapter 7—"Working Overseas for the United States Government."
   Chapter 8—"United States Non-Profit Organizations that Employ Personnel Abroad."
7. *Assistance to East Bengal and to Bengali Refugees in India.* New York: Technical Assistance Information Clearing House, December, 1971.
   This 28-page report includes descriptions of the work of sixty organizations.
8. *Black Portfolio.* Ed. Robert Mayhawk. New York: Robert Mayhawk Associates, 1970.
   A classified directory covering the black world of the arts, sciences, humanities, and business. Includes two sections on "Black Serving Organizations."
9. *Book of the States.* Supplement II; State Administrative Officials Classified by Functions. Ed. Robert H. Weber. Lexington, Ky.: Council of State Governments, 1971.
   A source for state agencies and officials concerned with: Aging, Community Affairs, Corrections, Drug Abuse Control, Economic Opportunity, Employment Security, Health, Human Rights, Juvenile Delinquency, Mental Hospitals and Community Mental Health, Mental Retardation, Natural Resources, Parole and Probation, Pollution Control, Public Assistance, and Welfare.
10. *Call for Action.* Compiled by WMCA: Call for Action. New York: New York Urban Coalition, 1970.
    Subject listing of public and private service agencies in New York City. Each entry gives: address and telephone numbers of

the agency; services provided; requirements of the agency; charges for services; and office hours of the agency.

11. CALVERT, ROBERT, JR. *Your Future in International Service.* New York: Richard Rosen Press, 1969.

12. CASEWIT, CURTIS W. *How to Get A Job Overseas.* New York: Arco Publishing Co., 1970.

13. *1971 Catalog of Federal Domestic Assistance.* Prepared by the Executive Office of the President, Office of Management and Budget. Washington, D.C.: Government Printing Office, 1971.
The *Catalog* is a comprehensive listing and description of federal programs and activities which provide assistance or benefits to the American public. It includes 1,069 programs administered by sixty-two different federal departments, independent agencies, commissions, and councils. Each program is described in terms of the specific type of assistance provided, the purpose for which it is available, who can apply for it, and how they should apply. It also identifies federal offices that can be contacted for additional information on the program.

14. CELLER, ROGER E. *The Challengers.* Washington, D.C.: Public Affairs Council, 1971.
A 29-page brochure listing alphabetically, within six broad classifications, organizations dedicated to changing the private sector of America. Included are civil rights, antiwar, consumer, ecology, Pro Bono Publico, and militant organizations. Gives addresses and descriptive commentary.

15. CHAMBERS, MERRITT MADISON. *Youth Serving Organizations—National Nongovernmental Associations.* Washington, D.C.: American Council on Education, 1948.

16. CLEMENTS, JOHN. *Taylor's Encyclopedia of Government Officials—Federal and State—Volume III 1971–1972.* Dallas: Political Research, Inc., 1971.

17. *College Placement Annual—1971.* Beth-

lehem, Penna.: College Placement Council, 1970.
The official occupational directory of the Regional Placement Associations, providing information on the positions customarily offered to college graduates by principal employers.

18. *Conservation Directory 1971.* Washington, D.C.: National Wildlife Federation, 1970.
A listing of organizations, agencies, and officials concerned with natural resource use and management.

19. *Directory—Correctional Institutions and Agencies of the United States of America, Canada and Great Britain 1971.* College Park, Md.: American Correctional Association, 1971.

20. *Directory—National Organizations with Programs in the Field of Aging 1971.* Washington, D.C.: National Council on the Aging, 1971.

21. *Directory of Agencies Serving the Visually Handicapped in the United States.* 17th ed. New York: American Foundation for the Blind, 1971.
A state-by-state listing of services on the state and local level with supplementary lists of specialized agencies and organizations, useful directories, and organizations with an interest in the blind.

22. *Directory of Comprehensive Neighborhood Health Service Programs.* Washington, D.C.: Office of Economic Opportunity, April, 1971.
Alphabetical listing, by state, of health programs. Gives addresses, director, and telephone number(s) for each program.

23. *Directory of Government Agencies Safeguarding Consumer and Environment 1972–73.* 4th ed. Alexandria, Va.: Serina Press, 1971.
Contains state-by-state listings of federal and/or state officials with jurisdiction in each state over Food and Drug, Meat and Poultry, Pesticides, Air Pollution Control, Water Pollution Control, Consumer Protection: Fraud and Deceptive Practices, Weights and Measures, Environmental

Control, Narcotics and Dangerous Drugs, and Noise Abatement Control.

24. *Directory of Human Rights Agencies (Public and Private) in New York City 1964.* New York: City of New York Commission on Human Rights, n.d.

25. *Directory of Intergroup Relations Agencies 1969.* Prepared by Brotherhood-In-Action, Inc. in cooperation with National Association of Intergroup Relations Officials. New York: Brotherhood-In-Action, 1969.

26. *1972 Directory of Member Agencies.* Compiled by FSAA Library. New York: Family Service Association of America, 1972.

27. *1972 Directory of Member Agencies and Associates.* 39th ed. New York: Child Welfare League of America, Inc., 1972.

28. *Directory of Organizations Concerned with Environmental Research.* Compiled by Wendell A. Mordy and Phyllis A. Sholtys. New York: State University College at Fredonia, 1970.
A computer-produced directory, international in scope. Organizations are listed both geographically and by the major field(s) of interest.

29. *Directory of Regional Social Welfare Activities.* Compiled by the Social Development Section of the Economic Commission for Africa. New York: United Nations, 1964.
International in scope.

30. *Directory of Schools, Agencies and Institutions for Children with Special Needs.* Ed. Alberta B. Turner. Columbus, Ohio: Ohio Youth Commission, 1968.

31. *Directory of Service Organizations.* Washington, D.C.: National Service Secretariat, 1968.
A listing of agencies—public, private and religious—that offer voluntary service opportunities for young people who are concerned with the war on poverty, on disease, on illiteracy, and on pollution.

32. *Directory of Social and Health Agencies of New York City—1971–1972.* Community Council of Greater New York, Inc. New York: Columbia University Press, 1971.
This directory provides information about voluntary and public welfare and health agencies serving New York City. Includes civic, educational, and religious organizations that offer services in the field of social welfare or in closely related fields. National agencies with offices in New York City, whose work is in the social and health field, are also listed.

33. *Directory of State and Local Resources for the Mentally Retarded.* Washington, D.C.: U.S. Department of Health, Education, and Welfare, 1970.

34. *Encyclopedia of Associations.* Vol. I. National Organizations of the United States. Ed. Margaret Fisk. Detroit: Gale Research, 1970.
Gives addresses, top officials, activities, and publications of U.S. organizations in every field of endeavor including: health and medical, labor, commerce, law, science, education, social welfare, public affairs, international affairs, and religion.

35. ———. Vol. 3, New Associations and Projects. No. 1, March, 1970. Detroit: Gale Research, 1970.

36. ———. Vol. 3, New Associations and Projects. No. 2, June, 1970. Detroit: Gale Research, 1970.

37. ———. Vol. 3, New Associations and Projects. No. 3, September, 1970. Detroit: Gale Research, 1970.

38. ———. Vol. 3, New Associations and Projects. No. 4, December, 1970. Detroit: Gale Research, 1970.

39. ———. Vol. 3, New Associations and Projects. No. 5, March, 1971. Detroit: Gale Research, 1971.

40. ———. Vol. 3, New Associations and Projects. No. 6, June, 1971. Detroit: Gale Research, 1971.

41. *Encyclopedia of Social Work.* 15th issue. New York: National Association of Social Workers, 1965.
In addition to subject articles and biographies, the encyclopedia contains a "Directory of Agencies" section, listing international agencies (voluntary and

intergovernmental); national governmental and voluntary agencies (U.S.); and Canadian governmental and voluntary agencies.

42. *Far East-Technical Assistance Programs of U.S. Non-Profit Organizations.* Ed. Mary Ellen Burgess. New York: Technical Assistance Information Clearing House, 1966.

43. *Federal Support for Adult Education: 1969 Directory of Programs and Services.* Prepared by the Adult Education Association of the U.S.A. New York: Macmillan, 1969.
This directory lists the agencies of the federal government that support or are engaged in adult or continuing education. It consists chiefly of brief descriptions of programs administered by those agencies that provide support or resources of various kinds for the field of adult education.

44. FORD, NORMAN D. *How to Travel and Get Paid For It;* 9th revised edition of *How to Get a Job that Takes You Travelling.* Greenlawn, N.Y.: Harian Publications, 1965.

45. FORRESTER, GERTRUDE. *Occupational Literature: An Annotated Bibliography.* New York: H. W. Wilson, 1971.

46. *Guide to Alternative Service.* Washington, D.C.: National Interreligious Service Board for Conscientious Objectors, March, 1970.
This guide is intended to serve as a source of general information on alternative service for both the individual conscientious objector and the counselor. It contains an alphabetical listing of agencies within four categories: state listings, federal government employment, special placement agencies, and foreign placement agencies.

47. ———. Part III: What Types of Work Can COs Do for Alternative Service? Washington, D.C.: National Interreligious Service Board for Conscientious Objectors, 1971.

48. ———. Part IV: Alternative Service Employers Listing. Washington, D.C.: National Interreligious Service Board for Conscientious Objectors, 1971.
Part III and Part IV are an interim updating of NISBCO's 1970 edition of *Guide to Alternative Service.*

49. *Guide to Information Sources in the Fields of Population Planning.* New York: Planned Parenthood-World Population, 1970.
A 16-page brochure. Includes a listing of pertinent organizations with their addresses.

50. *Handbook of National Organizations with Plans, Programs, and Services in the Field of Aging.* Washington, D.C.: Government Printing Office, 1960.

51. *Hotline* (1971–1972 numbers)
A weekly bulletin of current job opportunities for former ACTION volunteers, compiled by the Office of Voluntary Action Liaison.

52. *Information on Social Work Opportunities Abroad.* New York: National Assembly for Social Policy and Development, Inc., January, 1970.
A 6-page circular that outlines pertinent information on social work opportunities abroad and gives resources for making further inquiries.

53. *Intercom,* XI (May–June, 1969), 31–72.
This issue features "U.S. Voluntary Organizations and World Affairs." Gives the largest and most active organizations in the field, including a brief description of each organization with its address, an indication of the size of the staff, and the names of its executives.

54. *Intercom,* XII (March–April, 1970), 21–51.
This issue features "Careers in World Affairs."

55. *International Directory of Nation-Wide Organizations Concerned with Family, Youth and Child Welfare.* New York: United Nations, Department of Social Affairs, December, 1952.

56. *International Directory of Prisoners' Aid Agencies 1962.* Milwaukee: International Prisoners' Aid Association, 1962.

57. *Inventory of State and Areawide Health Planning Agencies and Related Organizations.* New York: Health Insurance Council, 1971.
Organized by states, this directory identifies the following in each state: state comprehensive health planning agency, HiCHAP coordinator, regional office of U.S.P.H.S., state health department, state mental health authority, hospital and medical facilities construction agency, regional medical program, community health planning agencies, and model cities program.

58. *Inventory of Youth Services in New York City.* New York: Human Resources Administration, March, 1969.

59. *Invest Yourself—1972.* New York: Commission on Voluntary Service & Action, 1971.
An annual publication listing several hundred voluntary service opportunities in the United States and abroad. Emphasis is on summer projects and nongovernmental agencies.

60. *iSVS Directory—Volunteer Sending Organizations: Central and Overseas Offices.* Washington, D.C.: International Secretariat for Volunteer Service, 1971.
Classified listing of organizations that are members of the International Secretariat for Volunteer Service (iSVS), an intergovernmental organization of fifty-two member countries working since 1962 for worldwide social and economic development by assisting and encouraging the creation, growth, and improvement of volunteer service organizations.

61. *Latin America-Technical Assistance Programs of U.S. Non-Profit Organizations.* Ed. Jane M. Meskill. New York: Technical Assistance Information Clearing House, 1967.

62. LEVITAN, SAR A. *Programs in Aid of the Poor for the 1970s.* Baltimore: John Hopkins Press, 1969.

63. *Listing of Sources for Employment Overseas.* New York: Division of Overseas Ministries, National Council of the Churches of Christ in the United States of America, May, 1971.
An 8-page booklet that gives information on opportunities for work with organizations involved in world affairs, including government, business, and the United Nations.

64. MARSHALL, MAX L. *Cowles Guide to Careers & Professions.* New York: Cowles Education Corp., 1968.

65. *Membership Directory.* The President's Committee on Employment of the Handicapped. Washington, D.C., October, 1966.

66. *Mental Health Directory 1971.* Rockville, Md.: National Institute of Mental Health, 1971.
A listing, by state, of nationally established agencies which provide mental health prevention, treatment, and rehabilitation services.

67. *National Directory of Private Social Agencies.* Compiled by Helen B. Croner. Ed. Kurt J. Guggenheimer. New York: Social Service Publications, 1964.
A loose-leaf directory of private social agencies in the United States, classified by services offered and listed by states and cities.

68. *1972 National Trade & Professional Associations of the United States & Buyers Guide.* Ed. Craig Colgate, Jr. Washington, D.C.: Columbia Books, 1972.

69. *Near East-South Asia Technical Assistance Programs of U.S. Non-Profit Organizations.* Ed. Barbro El Hakim. New York: Technical Assistance Information Clearing House, 1969.

70. *Nigeria-Assistance Programs of U.S. Non-Profit Organizations.* New York: Technical Assistance Information Clearing House, 1970.

71. OFFICE OF CONSUMER AFFAIRS. *Guide to Federal Consumer Services.* Washington, D.C.: Government Printing Office, 1971.
This guide lists the consumer services of thirty-four major departments and agencies and forty-one subagencies.

72. *Organizations Utilizing American Physi-*

cians Abroad. Washington, D.C.: Association of American Medical Colleges, 1971.
A 40-page booklet that lists government and private agencies that offer overseas service opportunities for physicians.

73. *Overseas Programs of Private Nonprofit American Organizations.* Compiled by the House Committee on Foreign Affairs. Washington, D.C.: Government Printing Office, 1965.

74. POWLEDGE, FRED. *New Careers; Real Jobs and Opportunity for the Disadvantaged.* New York: Public Affairs Committee, Inc., 1968. (Public Affairs Pamphlet No. 427.)

75. *Public Welfare Directory 1971.* Ed. Malvin Morton. 32nd ed. Chicago: American Public Welfare Association, 1971.
This directory outlines the administrative structure of public welfare and related programs at federal, state, and local levels. It gives the basic programs, practices, and staff of all public welfare and related public agencies in the United States and Canada. It also includes a description of International Social Service, lists certain international and national public and voluntary agencies that provide international social services; and list directories from ten national public and voluntary agencies.

76. *Regional Office Directory with Maps.* 2nd ed. Alexandria, Va.: Serina Press, 1971.
The directory provides the addresses and telephone numbers of the regional offices of forty selected federal agencies, along with thirty-eight jurisdictional maps.

77. *Service Directory of National Organizations 1971.* New York: National Assembly for Social Policy and Development, Inc., 1971.
This directory tells the purposes of 137 voluntary and governmental organizations, the services they give, and the channels through which these services may be obtained by local communities and organizations. Included are the names of the executives, the addresses and telephone numbers of the central offices, the listing of regional assignments with the names, addresses, and telephone

numbers of regional consultants.

78. SHILLER, ALICE. *The Unmarried Mother.* New York: Public Affairs Committee, Inc., 1969. (Public Affairs Pamphlet No. 440.)

79. *Sources of Medical Information.* Ed. Raphael Alexander. New York: Exceptional Books, 1969.
A guide to organizations and government agencies which are sources of information in the fields of medicine, health, disease, drugs, mental health, and related areas.

80. *South Vietnam-Assistance Programs of U.S. Non-Profit Organizations.* New York: Technical Assistance Information Clearing House, 1971.

81. *Special Catalog of Federal Programs Assisting Minority Enterprise—1971.* Prepared by the Office of Minority Business Enterprise. Washington, D.C.: Government Printing Office, Summer, 1971.
The catalog contains: descriptions of eighty-five federal programs which are either specifically designed to aid minority business enterprise, or which may be of particular help to minority entrepreneurs; a summary of seventy-five additional federal programs which directly or indirectly offer potential business opportunities; and the regional and field office locations of each federal agency responsible for administering the programs identified in the catalog.

82. *State Offices of Community Affairs;* their Functions, Organization and Enabling Legislation. Washington, D.C.: Council of State Governments, September, 1969.

83. *TAICH News,* No. 23, Fall 1970.

84. ———. No. 24, Winter 1971.

85. ———. No. 25, Spring 1971.

86. ———. No. 26, January 1972.
TAICH News is issued by the Technical Assistance Information Clearing House. The Clearing House serves as a center of information on the socio-economic development programs abroad of U.S. voluntary agencies, missions, and foundations and other nonprofit organizations.

87. *Teaching Abroad.* New York: Institute of International Education, August, 1971.

A 22-page circular that gives information on organizations which administer teacher exchange programs, hire teachers for overseas assignments, or provide informational services for teachers seeking jobs abroad.

88. *Teaching Opportunities in Latin America for U.S. Citizens.* Washington, D.C.: General Secretariat, Organization of American States, August, 1970.
A 9-page circular covering pertinent agencies.

89. *To Tell the Truth.* Chicago: Cooperative League of the USA, n.d.
An illustrated outline of some of the consumer information and protection activities of American cooperatives.

90. *Transition,* December, 1971.

91. ———. January, 1972.

92. ———. February, 1972.
A magazine for former ACTION volunteers published by the Office of Voluntary Action Liaison. This office assists former volunteers with their educational and career development.

93. UNITED NATIONS EDUCATIONAL, SCIENTIFIC AND CULTURAL ORGANIZATION. *Teaching Abroad/Enseignement à l'étranger.* Geneva, Switzerland: Imprimeries Populaires, 1970.
This 62-page brochure is intended to help teachers and other qualified persons wishing to teach in another country for a limited period to find opportunities to do so. It contains information on agencies and organizations in eighty-three countries concerned in one way or another with the recruitment of staff for teaching assignments abroad.

94. *United States Department of Justice—Directory of Organizations Serving Minority Communities.* Washington, D.C.: Government Printing Office, 1971.
A directory of names and addresses of some organizations throughout the country that are involved in serving minority communities.

95. *United States Government Organization Manual 1971/72.* Washington, D.C.: Government Printing Office, 1971.
The official organization handbook of the federal government. It describes the creation and authority, organization, functions, and current officials of the agencies in the legislative, judicial, and executive branches; it also provides brief descriptions of boards, commissions, committees, quasi-official agencies, and selected international agencies. A "Sources of Information" section, included in most agency statements, gives helpful information to those interested in employment with the federal government.

96. U.S. CIVIL SERVICE COMMISSION. *Federal Jobs Overseas.* Washington, D.C.: Government Printing Office, July, 1970.
This 12-page pamphlet lists the principal agencies that have personnel outside the United States, indicates the kinds of positions for which they may be recruiting, and lists the addresses to which inquiries or applications should be sent.

97. ———. *Guide to Federal Career Literature.* Washington, D.C.: Government Printing Office, 1971.
This 30-page directory is designed to serve as a convenient reference guide to federal recruiting literature. It contains brief descriptions of 224 publications from forty-six different departments and agencies. The pamphlets and brochures listed represents only the principal publications used in nationwide recruiting for college entry-level positions.

98. U.S. COMMISSION ON CIVIL RIGHTS. *Civil Rights Directory 1970.* Washington, D.C.: Government Printing Office, n.d.
This directory consists of five sections: (1) Officials of thirty-eight federal agencies who are responsible for monitoring, administering, coordinating, and enforcing various aspects of equal opportunity laws and policies; (2) Federal officials with liaison responsibility for programs of special interest to Spanish-speaking groups; (3) National private organizations with civil rights programs; (4) Official state agencies with civil rights responsibilities; and (5) County and municipal commissions with civil rights responsibilities.

99. U.S. DEPARTMENT OF HEALTH, EDUCA-

TION, AND WELFARE. *Directory—Poison Control Centers.* Washington, D.C.: Food and Drug Administration, Bureau of Product Safety, March, 1971.

Gives the name, address, and director of the facilities, alphabetically by state, which provide for the medical profession, on a twenty-four-hour basis, information concerning the treatment and prevention of accidents involving ingestion of poisonous and potentially poisonous substances.

100. ———. *Volunteer Opportunities for Social Workers.* Washington, D.C.: Government Printing Office, n.d.

An 8-page brochure covering sixteen private organizations and government agencies offering overseas positions.

101. U.S. DEPARTMENT OF LABOR. *Occupational Outlook Handbook 1970–71 Edition.* Washington, D.C.: Government Printing Office, n.d.

This handbook contains accurate career information for use in guidance. It gives the latest and the most authoritative and specific information possible covering the nature of work, education and training requirements, employment outlook, places of employment, and earnings and working conditions for over 700 occupations.

102. *U.S. Non-Profit Organizations, Voluntary Agencies, Missions and Foundations Participating in Technical Assistance Abroad.* Ed. Dao N. Spencer. New York: Technical Assistance Information Clearing House, 1964.

103. ———. *Supplement 1965.* Ed. Binnie Schroyer. New York: Nuko Incorp., 1965.

104. *VISTA Fact Book.* Washington, D.C.: ACTION, September, 1971.

The ACTION/VISTA Fact Book was compiled to provide current information on VISTA Volunteers and sponsoring organizations. It gives the names of project contacts along with the addresses and telephone numbers of VISTA's local sponsors. All active projects are included. It is arranged alphabetically by state and, within each state, by the type of project. A brief description of Volunteer activities is included for each project.

105. *Vocations for Social Change,* July–August, 1971.

A bimonthly journal which contains current information on: new social change projects; staff openings in existing organizations; how and why people have created specific social change projects; and both national and regional sources of information on particular areas of change such as health, media, women's liberation, etc. In addition, each issue focuses on an area of current interest; this issue covers "health care."

106. ———. September–October, 1971.

Special feature articles devoted to "communes and collectives."

107. ———. November–December, 1971.

Feature articles on "prisons."

108. ———. January–February, 1972.

Feature articles on "gay people."

109. ———. March–April, 1972.

This issue has special articles on "community organizing as a means by which to strengthen the sense of struggle and eliminate poverty."

Continued by *Work Force.*

110. WASSERMAN, CLARA SEDACCA, AND PAUL WASSERMAN. *Health Organizations of the United States and Canada: National, Regional and State.* Ithaca, N.Y.: Cornell University, 1961.

A directory of voluntary associations, professional societies, and other groups concerned with health and related fields.

111. *Work Force,* May–June, 1972.

Continues *Vocations for Social Change;* this issue covers the theme of "visual media."

112. *Yearbook of International Organizations;* 13th (1970–71) Edition. Ed. R. A. Hall. Brussels, Belgium: Union of International Associations, 1971.

An annotated directory of international voluntary organizations in all fields of endeavor. Descriptions of each organization's aims and work are given, along with addresses, size, officers, and structure.

PART V

Indexes

Function Index

Abortion. *See* Family Planning
Addiction. *See* Alcoholism; Narcotics—Addiction and Control
Adolescents. *See* Youth—Programs and Services
Africa—Programs
    Agricultural Cooperative Development International
    American Friends of the Middle East
    Board of Missions of the United Methodist Church
    Catholic Relief Services
    Near East Foundation
    World Education
    Department of State/Agency for International Development
Aged
    Salvation Army
    Minnesota/Department of Public Welfare
    South Carolina/State Department of Public Welfare
    West Virginia/Department of Welfare
Agriculture—Programs and Services
    Agricultural Cooperative Development International
    International Voluntary Services
    Department of Agriculture/Extension Service
    Department of Agriculture/Farmer Cooperative Service
    Department of State/Agency for International Development
    ACTION/Peace Corps
Alcoholism
    California/Department of Rehabilitation
    Delaware/Division of Drug Abuse
    Texas/Texas Rehabilitation Commission
Asia—Programs
    Agricultural Cooperative Development International
    Board of Missions of the United Methodist Church

    Catholic Relief Services
    Department of State/Agency for International Development

Birth Control. *See* Family Planning
Birth Defects
    National Foundation-March of Dimes
Business Advice and Financial Aid. *See* Economic Development and Opportunities

Child Welfare
    Alaska Children's Services
    Florence Crittenton Home and Services
    Foster Parents Plan
    Robert F. Kennedy Memorial
    Salvation Army
    ACTION/Foster Grandparent Program
    Alabama/Department of Pensions and Security
    Alaska/Department of Health and Social Services
    Connecticut/Department of Children and Youth Services
    Kentucky/Department of Child Welfare
    Minnesota/Department of Public Welfare
    South Carolina/State Department of Public Welfare
    West Virginia/Department of Welfare
Civil Rights
    NAACP Legal Defense and Educational Fund
    Department of Justice/Community Relations Service
    U.S. Commission on Civil Rights
    Indiana/Civil Rights Commission
    Kentucky/Commission on Human Rights
    Michigan/Civil Rights Commission
Community Affairs
    Department of Justice/Community Relations Service

Connecticut/Department of Community Affairs

Pennsylvania/Department of Community Affairs

Virginia/Division of State Planning and Community Affairs

Community Development

Department of Housing and Urban Development

California/Department of Housing and Community Development

Ohio/Community Economic Improvement Group

Conscientious Objectors

Central Committee for Conscientious Objectors

Conservation. *See also* Forests; Pollution Control

Environmental Defense Fund

Friends of the Earth

The Nature Conservancy

Public Interest Research Group

Department of Agriculture/Forest Service

Department of Agriculture/Soil Conservation Service

Department of the Interior/Bureau of Land Management

Department of the Interior/National Park Service

ACTION/Smithsonian Institution-Peace Corps Environmental Program

Alabama/Department of Conservation and Natural Resources

California/Department of Conservation

Michigan/Department of Natural Resources

New York/Department of Environmental Conservation

Virginia/Department of Conservation and Economic Development

Consumer—Programs and Services

Center for Auto Safety

Council of Better Business Bureaus

Health Research Group

Public Interest Research Group

Department of Health, Education, and Welfare/Food and Drug Administration

Federal Trade Commission

Cooperatives

Agricultural Cooperative Development International

Foundation for Cooperative Housing

Department of Agriculture/Farmer Cooperative Service

Crime/Correctional Care and Services

National Council on Crime and Delinquency

Pennsylvania Prison Society

Salvation Army

Department of Justice/Bureau of Prisons

Alaska/Department of Health and Social Services

California/Department of Corrections

Connecticut/Department of Children and Youth Services

Kentucky/Department of Corrections

Maryland/Department of Juvenile Services

Day Care Centers. *See* Child Welfare

Disaster Relief

American National Red Cross

Catholic Relief Services

Direct Relief Foundation

Department of Agriculture/Food and Nutrition Service

Alabama/Department of Pensions and Security

West Virginia/Department of Welfare

Discrimination. *See* Civil Rights

Drug Addiction. *See* Narcotics—Addiction and Control

Economic Development and Opportunities

Business and Job Development Corporation

Dallas Alliance for Minority Enterprise

Inter-American Development Bank

Department of Commerce/Office of Minority Business Enterprise

Small Business Administration

Ohio/Community Economic Improvement Group

Pennsylvania/Department of Community Affairs

Education and Teaching

American Field Service International Scholarships

American Friends of the Middle East

Foreign Policy Association

Near East College Association

People, Incorporated

World Education

Department of Agriculture/Extension Service

Department of Health, Education, and Welfare/Office of Education/- Teacher Corps

200

Indexes

National Tuberculosis and Respiratory Disease Association
Pan American Sanitary Bureau
People-to-People Health Foundation/-Project HOPE
Project Concern
Salvation Army
Department of Health, Education, and Welfare/Food and Drug Administration
Department of Labor/Occupational Safety and Health Administration
Alaska/Department of Health and Social Services
Minnesota/Department of Public Welfare
Missouri/Division of Health
North Carolina/State Board of Health
Oklahoma/State Department of Health

Homeless
Salvation Army

Housing
Foundation for Cooperative Housing
Department of Housing and Urban Development
California/Department of Housing and Community Development
Connecticut/Department of Community Affairs

International Exchange
American Field Service International Scholarships
American Friends of the Middle East

Job Training. *See* Employment and Vocational Programs and Services

Juvenile Delinquents. *See* Crime/Correctional Care and Services; Youth—Programs and Services

Latin America—Programs
Agricultural Cooperative Development International
Board of Missions of the United Methodist Church
Catholic Relief Services
Inter-American Development Bank
International Development Foundation
Pan American Sanitary Bureau
World Education
Department of State/Agency for International Development

Law
International Legal Center
Public Interest Research Group
Federal Trade Commission

Legal Aid
California Rural Legal Assistance
Migrant Legal Action Program
NAACP Legal Defense and Educational Fund

Literacy Programs. *See* Education and Teaching

Maternity Services. *See also* Family Planning; Family—Programs and Services
Florence Crittenton Home and Services
Salvation Army

Medical. *See* Health and Medical Programs and Services

Mental Health—Programs and Services
Alaska Children's Services
People, Incorporated
Alaska/Department of Health and Social Services
California/Department of Rehabilitation
Kentucky/Department of Child Welfare
Michigan/Department of Mental Health
Minnesota/Department of Public Welfare
Vermont/Department of Mental Health

Middle East—Programs
American Friends of the Middle East
Near East College Association
Near East Foundation

Minority Groups—Programs and Services
Americans for Indian Opportunity
Business and Job Development Corporation
Dallas Alliance for Minority Enterprise
Joint Action in Community Service
Migrant Legal Action Program
Opportunities Industrialization Center
Department of Commerce/Office of Minority Business Enterprise
Department of Justice/Community Relations Service
New Jersey/Department of Labor and Industry
Ohio/Community Economic Improvement Group

Narcotics—Addiction and Control
DO IT NOW Foundation
Salvation Army
Department of Justice/Bureau of Narcotics and Dangerous Drugs
Delaware/Division of Drug Abuse

Retarded
 Michigan/Department of Mental Health
 Minnesota/Department of Public Welfare
Runaways. *See* Child Welfare; Youth—Programs and Services
Rural Development. *See also* Agriculture—Programs and Services
 International Development Foundation
 International Voluntary Services
 Lutheran World Relief
 Near East Foundation
 Department of Agriculture/Extension Service
 Department of State/Agency for International Development
 ACTION/Peace Corps

Safety
 American National Red Cross
 Center for Auto Safety
 Department of Labor/Occupational Safety and Health Administration
 Department of Transportation/National Highway Traffic Safety Administration
 Alabama/Department of Conservation and Natural Resources
 New Jersey/Department of Labor and Industry
Sanitation. *See* Pollution Control
Scholarships. *See* Education and Teaching
Seamen/Servicemen
 American National Red Cross
 Central Committee for Conscientious Objectors
 United Seamen's Service
Social Services
 International Social Service, American Branch
 Salvation Army
 Alabama/Department of Pensions and Security
 Alaska/Department of Health and Social Services
 Kentucky/Department of Economic Security
 Minnesota/Department of Public Welfare
 South Carolina/State Department of Public Welfare
 West Virginia/Department of Welfare
Teaching. *See* Education and Teaching
Technical Assistance. *See* Overseas Assistance and Programs

Unemployed. *See* Employment and Vocational Programs and Services
Unmarried Parents
 Florence Crittenton Home and Services
 Salvation Army
 Kentucky/Department of Child Welfare
Urban Development
 Department of Housing and Urban Development
 Connecticut/Department of Community Affairs
 Pennsylvania/Department of Community Affairs

Venereal Disease. *See* Health and Medical Programs and Services
Veterans
 American National Red Cross

Welfare—Programs and Services. *See also* Child Welfare
 Alabama/Department of Pensions and Security
 Alaska/Department of Health and Social Services
 Kentucky/Department of Economic Security
 Minnesota/Department of Public Welfare
 South Carolina/State Department of Public Welfare
 West Virginia/Department of Welfare
Wildlife Management. *See* Conservation; Forests

Youth—Programs and Services
 Alaska Children's Service
 American Field Service International Scholarships
 American National Red Cross
 Big Brothers of America
 Boys' Clubs of America
 Encampment for Citizenship
 Girl Scouts of the U.S.A.
 People, Incorporated
 ACTION/Foster Grandparent Program
 Connecticut/Department of Children and Youth Services
 Delaware/Division of Youth Affairs
 Kentucky/Department of Child Welfare
 Maryland/Department of Juvenile Services

Occupation Index

Directors (Overseas Educational Program), 13
Directors (Overseas Program), 29, 43
Directors (Personnel Management and Rehabilitation), 48
Directors (Public Welfare Program), 135, 177
Directors (Youth Program), 23, 46
Disaster Representatives, 17
District Directors (Health Program), 66
Doctors. *See* Physicians
Doctors Assistants, 83
Draft and Military Counselors, 31
Drug Counselors, 37, 146. *See also* Addiction Counselors

Economists, 53, 120, 128, 167
Economists (Agricultural), 98, 118
Education Advisers (Overseas Program), 118
Educational Directors (Youth Program), 24
Educational Services Specialists, 12, 13
Educators, 46, 53, 98, 112, 120, 168. *See also* Instructors; Teachers
Educators (Correctional Program), 151
Educators (Health Program), 79, 136, 161, 170
Eligibility Specialists (Public Welfare Program), 185
Employment Counselors, 77, 137, 148, 153, 162, 165. *See also* Counselors
Employment Interviewers, 148, 153, 162
Employment Service Advisers, 116
Enforcement Analysts (Environmental Protection Program), 126
Engineers, 31, 53, 100, 118, 120, 126, 154, 184
Entomologists, 79, 100, 126
Environmental Engineers, 136, 154
Executive Directors (Health Program), 14, 20, 71, 73
Executive Directors (Rehabilitation Program), 48
Executive Directors (Youth Program), 23, 46
Explosives Safety Inspectors, 165

Fellows. *See* Fellowships
Fellowships, 50, 56, 62
Field Directors (Immigration Program), 11
Field Directors (Overseas Program), 16, 43
Field Representatives (Health Program), 14, 71, 73
Field Representatives (Overseas Program), 51, 89
Field Representatives (Social Services Program), 17

Field Workers (Public Welfare Program), 153
Food Marketing Specialists, 99
Food Stamp Field Representatives, 153
Food Stamp Workers, 153
Food Technologists, 99
Forest Engineers, 184
Foresters, 100, 108, 167, 181, 184
Forest Product Technologists, 100
Forest Rangers, 167
Forestry Aides, 181
Forestry Assistants, 181
Forestry Technicians, 167
Forest Wardens, 181
Foster Grandparents, 120, 180
Fund Raisers, 14, 20, 31, 46, 73, 74

Game Area Managers, 134, 158
Grant Specialists, 164
Group Club Supervisors (Youth Program), 24
Group Counselors, 9
Group Workers, 87
Guide Dog Instructors, 49

Health Administrators, 170
Health Officers, 161, 176
Health Program Representatives, 161
Home Economists, 99
Home Health Aides, 174
Homemakers, 177
Hospital Administrators (Overseas Program), 64
Hospital Aides, 160
Hospital Recreation Workers, 16
Housemothers, 9
Housing and Redevelopment Analysts, 174
Housing Development Specialists, 44
Housing Management Specialists, 106
Human Resources Development Specialists, 174
Human Rights Representatives, 149
Human Rights Workers, 39
Hydraulic Engineers, 167

Industrial Hygiene Engineers, 170
Industrial Hygiene Technicians, 170
Industrial Hygienists, 117
Inspectors (Food and Drug Program), 103
Instructors (Employment Program), 78, 137
Instructors (Health Education), 136
Instructors (Medical), 36
Instructors (Nursing), 64, 79
Instructors (Vocational), 137, 143
Instructors. *See also* Educators; Teachers
Investigators (Civil Rights Program), 147
Investigators (Legal Program), 26

Indexes

Investigators (Public Health Program), 170

Job Developers, 78, 137
Job Development Specialists (Rehabilitation Program), 142
Juvenile Counselors, 150
Juvenile Probation Workers, 155

Laboratory Technicians, 85
Land Surveyors, 184
Lands Inspectors, 134
Landscape Architects, 100, 106. *See also* Architects
Law Clerks, 65
Lawyers. *See* Attorneys
Licensed Practical Nurses, 173
Loan and Technical Assistance Specialists (Overseas Program), 51

Management Specialists (Food Program), 99
Management Trainees (Consumer Program), 33
Manpower Development Specialists, 116
Mathematicians, 120
Medical Consultants, 142
Medical Officers, 79, 104. *See also* Physicians
Medical Social Work Consultants, 160, 176
Medical Social Workers, 70, 137, 176, 177
Medical Technicians/Technologists, 27, 38, 41, 62, 64, 82, 118
Metropolitan Development Specialists, 106
Microbiologists, 104, 136, 161
Migrant Labor Inspectors, 165
Mining Safety Inspectors, 165
Model Cities Specialists, 107

Narcotic Correction Officers, 168
Narcotic Parole Officers, 169
Narcotic Rehabilitation Counselors, 168
Neighborhood Health Visitors, 173
Neighborhood Resource Workers, 145
Nurses, 17, 27, 34, 36, 38, 39, 41, 48, 58, 62, 64, 79, 82, 83, 85, 87, 118, 136, 157, 160, 161, 168, 170, 173, 176, 179, 180. *See also* Licensed Practical Nurses; Rehabilitation Nurses
Nurse-midwives, 83
Nursing Consultants, 17, 72, 176
Nutrition Aides, 180
Nutritionists, 161, 170. *See also* Dietitians

Occupational Therapists, 48, 70, 87, 160

Operations Directors (Rehabilitation Program), 48
Organizers (Cooperative Program), 98
Outdoor Recreation Planners, 109

Paramedical Personnel, 27, 36, 64, 82
Park Aides, 110
Park Guides, 110
Park Managers, 134
Park Rangers, 110, 134, 158, 181
Park Technicians, 110
Parole Agents, 140
Patient Service Coordinators, 66
Pharmacists, 85, 112
Pharmacologists, 112
Physical Directors (Youth Program), 24
Physical Therapists, 48, 64, 69, 82, 160, 170
Physicians, 22, 27, 36, 38, 41, 50, 62, 64, 82, 83, 85, 87, 104, 112, 118, 120, 136, 151, 157, 160, 168, 170, 176, 179. *See also* Health Officers; Medical Officers; Psychiatrists
Physicists, 120, 126
Physiotherapists, 62
Placement Interviewers (Rehabilitation Program), 61
Placement Specialists (Rehabilitation Program), 178
Planning Analysts (Community Affairs Program), 175
Plant Pathologists, 100
Plant Scientists, 59
Probation and Parole Officers, 151
Probation Officers, 136,
Program Advisers (Youth Program), 147
Program Assistants (Overseas Program), 29
Program Associates (Health Program), 73
Program Consultants (Health Program), 73
Program Coordinators (OEO Program), 164
Program Directors (Health Program), 66
Program Directors (Overseas Program), 29
Program Directors (Youth Program), 24, 46
Psychiatric Social Workers, 137
Psychiatrists, 48, 87, 168, 180
Psychologists, 48, 70, 87, 120, 137, 143, 151, 157, 168, 173, 180
Public Health Community Workers, 173
Public Health Nurses. *See* Nurses
Public Health Nursing Consultants, 170, 176
Public Health Physicians. *See* Physicians
Public Health Program Specialists, 126
Public Relations Specialists, 14, 20, 46, 48, 74